101 & ½ Raw Zucchinis
and What to Do with Them

2nd Edition
with new and improved plant-based raw food recipes

by

Kachina Choate
Summer Bear

Tuna Wrap

101 & ½ Raw Zucchinis & What to Do with Them

Copyright © 2019 Kachina Choate

All Rights reserved. No part of this publication may be reproduced, stored in a retrieval system, or transmitted, in any form by any means, electronic, mechanical, photocopying, recording, or otherwise, without the prior written consent of the copyright owner.

frontdesk@summerbear.org

First Printing March, 2006
Second Edition Printing, 2019

Library of Congress Control Number: 2019911541

ISBN 978-1-938142-00-0 (print)
ISBN 978-1-938142-01-7 (eBook)

1. Raw Foods 2. Cookery (Natural foods)

Thank you, Tamara, for editing.

This book is not intended to cure or give medical advice. Its intention is to educate, inform, and empower readers to make their own decisions on health and well-being. Each person will have unique reactions to changes in diet. If you have concerns about your health or diet, consult your healthcare advisor.

Table of Contents

4	Introduction
5	The Incredible Zucchini
15	Soups & Salad Recipes
49	Side & Main Dish Recipes
87	Dessert Recipes
101	Miscellaneous Recipes
117	Appendix
125	Index

Introduction

When I grew zucchinis in my garden, neighbors would reluctantly ask if I wanted more, I always accepted. After a while, they asked, "what do you do with all of those zucchinis?" After sharing a couple of my recipes, they loved and enjoyed. They no longer had extra zucchini to share with me.

When I no longer had a garden and the neighbors no longer shared zucchini. I was told 'everyone has lots of zucchini just leave your car unlocked in the church parking lot and it will be filled with zucchini. I drove my car to a parking lot and left it. Upon returning there were no zucchinis.

Later I leaned August 8th is Sneak a Zucchini onto Your Neighbor's Porch Night, it really is. So, with bated breath I put up a sign saying, "Zucchinis Welcome!!!" Much to my dismay none were delivered. I guess I was a little too hasty sharing my recipes with the neighbors.

There are so many reasons to become thrilled about squash. Zucchini is a wonderful, versatile vegetable that can be featured and added to make anything from a main dish to a dessert. Zucchinis can extend meals and reduce caloric intake so, they can be great for the waist line too.

I was watching a TV chef and he refer to a zucchini as boring, my mouth dropped to the ground. He obviously does not understand the incredible zucchini.

I totally agree with actress Gwyneth Paltrow's declaration;

> *"When I pass a flowering zucchini plant in a garden, my heart skips a beat."*

With these recipes I hope to make your heart skip a beat. Remember when you make your own food you are in charge. Mix it up switch it out add to the recipe change it as you like.

Enjoy the incredibly versatile, edible zucchini.

The Incredible Zucchini

Zucchini A Brief History

The zucchini is classified as a summer squash and is in season beginning mid-July through mid-August in most North American climates. Squashes are native to the Americas and belongs to the curcurbita family. While zucchini is botanically a fruit in the culinary world, it is treated as a vegetable.

The name squash was adapted from several Native American words meaning "something eaten raw." South Americas call zucchini "baby marrow."

Archaeological evidence of zucchini is found as far back and 7,000 years ago in South America. In Mexico the main home of zucchini, they were an integral part of their diet of maize, beans, and squashes.

Today, zucchini is widely-recognized and is a favorite of home gardeners. It's easy to care for and grows in most areas of the country during the summer.

Christopher Columbus introduced this exotic vegetable to Europe and the Mediterranean region. The Italians embraced the it fully. In fact, the name "zucchini" originated in Italy. However, it wasn't used in its current form until the late 1800s or early 1900s;

The French didn't care much for courgetti, as they call it until their chefs discovered smaller zucchini had better flavor than large overgrown zucchini.

It is believed that the Italian immigrants brought the zucchini back to North America in the 1920s. Zucchini is on record along with 60 other vegetables grown in New York State in 1928.

Zucchini is known by many names is enjoyed all over the world.

Mexicans use it in soups and quesadillas. French use

it in ratatouille and courgette farchi (a stew of zucchini with tomatoes or bell peppers.) Turkish use it in mücver a pancake like dish. Egyptians eat it with tomato sauce, garlic and onions. Bulgarians fry zucchini and serve it with a yogurt dip.

Wither zucchini is dipped in a special sauce at a party or sliced in a salad or blended in a main dish or dessert I hope you too fall in love and enjoy eating it.

Picking Zucchini

When choosing zucchini look for ones with a sound exterior and avoid those with nicks, pits, and bruises or soft spots.

The skin should be plump (not shriveled), stem ends fresh and green, and the color should be bright and uniform.

Zucchini tastes best when it is not more than seven (7) inches long. The bigger they are, the bigger the seeds, and the more coarse and stringy the flesh.

Types of Zucchini

There are many types of zucchini including:

Round Zucchini:

'**Golden Egg**' zucchini is another yellow skin zucchini but is shaped like elongated eggs.

'**Round De Nice**' are round dark-skinned zucchini.

Heirloom Zucchini:

'**Black Beauty**' this zucchini is one of the most popular varieties. It is cylindrical in shape.

'**Fodhook**' is smooth cylindrical zucchini with mottled green skin and the creamy white flesh has a good texture.

'**Golden Rush**' which have a deep yellow skin and a dark green stem. Its favor is sweeter than that of green verities.

'**Cocozelle**' zucchini has dark green streaks. It is tender and are very good used when stuffing zucchini.

'**Caserta**' produces a light greenish-grey zucchini with darker green stripes and had good flavor.

Hybrid Zucchini:

'**Raven**' are deep green and loaded with an antioxidant, leutein, that helps protect the eyes from UV damage.

'**Dunja**' produces dark green straight zucchinis.

'**Gadzukes**' is dark green with light green ridges and slices slightly star-shapes.

'**Magda**' is a squat zucchini with pale green skin. At Johnny's taste trials. It earned best middle-eastern squash flavor with a dense, nutty-tasting flesh.

'**Summer Green Tiger**' had bold dark green strips and Burpee Seed voted it the best-looking and best-tasting zucchini.

'**Bush Baby**' is a squat and ideal harvest size is 2 inches by 6 inches. The compact plant is one of the best zucchini varieties for growing in containers.

'**Patio Star**' is bread specifically for growing in containers and are easy to harvest.

Refrigerated:

Keep the squash whole, dry and unwashed. Store them in a plastic or paper bag opened at one end to encourage air circulation.

Zucchini rots when it comes in contact with too much moisture, so make sure to keep it in the crisper drawer. They'll keep in the refrigerator for 1 to 2 weeks, though you'll probably see the skin start to shrivel over time.

Frozen:

To freeze zucchini cut it in chunks or shred and pack into a freezer bag or container. Zucchini will keep for about 3 months in the freezer. The texture will change when frozen and thawed. The best place to use frozen zucchini is in soups.

Dehydrated:

To dehydrate zucchini slice or shred it then place in a single layer on the drying trays and dry at about 100° F for about 12 hours. Once dehydrated the should be crisp.

Preserve in airtight containers until you're ready to use. Dried squash has a shelf life of up to two years and should be rotated.

Freeze Dried:

Freeze dried zucchini is another way to store zucchini for food storage. This method will last zucchini for 5-10 years when properly sealed and stored.

When I dry or freeze dry zucchini I like to grate, slice or zoodle it into whatever shape I think I will use. Zucchini dried into the shape you want makes it easier to use when needed in soup, salad, main dish or sweet.

Zucchini Blossoms

Many consider squash blossoms a delicacy. They are yellow-orange flowers, which appear first on the vines that produce the squash and may be eaten fresh.

The most tender blossoms are the ones that are picked the day are about to open for the first time. Blossoms should be opened and inspected for bugs, which can be gently rinsed with water to clean.

When you choose blossoms, the female flowers are succulent, soft and fleshy and have a small fruit attached to the stem end. The male flowers, the ones without fruit attached, are hairier.

Zucchini blossoms are traditionally served battered and

deep-fried, which adds fat and calories. Raw zucchini blossoms are a health-supportive addition to any summertime meal. They also make a wonderful garnish for soups, rice, and salads.

Zucchini Nutrition

3 ½ ounces zuchhini raw (¾ cup sliced)

Calories	14
Carbohydrate	3 g
Dietary Fiber	Low
Cholesterol	0 mg
Protein	1g
Saturated Fat	< 1 g
Fat	<1 g
Sodium	3 mg

Key Nutrients		%RDA Men	%RDA Women
Vitamin C	9mg	15%	15%
Folacin	22 mg	11%	12%

Zucchinis offers valuable antioxidants and trace amounts of B-vitamins, folic acid, and calcium.

Zucchini blossoms are a good source of vitamins, nutrients, and minerals responsible for boosting immunity and overall heart health and supporting bone density and healthy skin and eyes. They are low in calories and a good source of beta- carotene, Vitamin C and Potassium, and their flavor faintly resembles that of the squash.

Interestingly when zucchini is cooked the calories increase to 18 compared to 14 for the same quantity of raw.

Traditional Therapeutic Benefits of Zucchini

It is believed that Hippocrates said "let food be thy medicine, and medicine be thy food."

While this is interesting, do zucchinis really have any health impact? The short answer is 'yes.'

It is believed that zucchini has a wide range of therapeutic properties which can help with digestion, weight loss and heart conditions.

Zucchinis have a cooling nature and a diuretic affect. for these two reasons it is believed to be beneficial for gastritis, indigestion, colitis and irritable bowel.

Zucchinis are heart healthy too, they are a prominent part of the DASH diet, also called Dietary Approaches to Stop Hypertension, aimed at improving heart health. Some people recommend zucchini to aid in cases of hypertension, arteriosclerosis and coronary disease.

While zucchini has relatively high protein, content they have very little fat and calories. Which is why many people use them int their diets for weight loss.

Zucchini is rich in lutein and zeaxanthin, two antioxidants found to prevent age-related macular degeneration of the eyes.

Zucchinis are also a good source of vitamin A which is important for eye development and maintenance. A report published by Flaum Eye Institute at the University of Rochester Medical Center indicates a low-fat diet could be beneficial for the eyes

The lutein, zeaxanthin and vitamin K in zucchini also keep bones and teeth strong. In addition, they also strengthen blood cells.

Zucchini is rich in magnesium is another nutrient works along with calcium to improve muscle contraction.

They are also rich in manganese, a mineral that promotes optimal functioning of the thyroid gland.

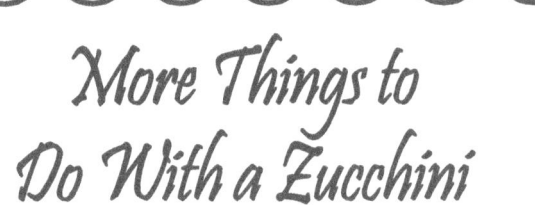

More Things to Do With a Zucchini

1. Practice juggling skills.

2. Learn to whittle
   There is less chance of harming yourself because unlike wood zucchinis are easy to care and shape without sharp knives.

3. Make center pieces and other decorations

4. Teething toy for baby
   Wash the skin of the zucchini and place in the freezer. When baby needs something cold to chew on give the. **It is important to make sure the zucchini remains frozen.** When it thaws pieces, can be bitten off and depending on the size could be a choking hazard.

3. Make animal art.
   Carve the zucchini to look like animals using toothpicks to add parts such as eyes, legs etc... This is a great activity to do at parties.

4. Share
    a. Give recipes to friends along with zucchini
    b. Make a zucchini gift basket.
        i. Get a basket place copy of this book along with zucchinis and a packet of seeds or a zucchini start. Or pick enough zucchinis to fill a basket. Then place a copy of this book in with it and wrap it up in something nice.
        ii. Pick a zucchini recipe and buy all the ingredients. Place the ingredients and recipe in basket.
        iii. Make several zucchini items place them in a basket with a copy of this book.
        iv. Find kitchen items that are in the shape of zucchini or have zucchinis on it. Place them in a basket.
    c. Don't forget that August 8th is Sneak a Zucchini Onto Your Neighbor's Porch Night!

Soups & Salads

Buttered Zucchini

Vegetable "Noodle" Soup

Makes 4-6 Servings

Preparation Time:
30
Minutes

This soup is a good substitute for chicken noodle soup when you are not feeling well.

Vegetable "Noodle" Soup

Ingredients

Soup Base

- 2 c. pure water
- tsp. cold pressed olive oil
- ½ c. celery, chopped
- ½ c. onion, chopped
- ¼ tsp. poultry seasoning
- 2 tsp. himalayan crystal salt or sea salt
- ½ tsp. white pepper

"Noodles"

- ½ c. celery, sliced
- 1 c. carrot, cut into thin slices
- 1 c. zucchini, shredded to look like 'spaghetti'
- ½ c. corn, fresh or frozen cut off the cob
- ½ c. broccoli, cut into bite-sized pieces

Directions

In a blender, blend the soup base ingredients until smooth. Add enough water to make the texture and thickness you desire. Set aside.

Prepare "noodles" by thinly slicing celery and chopping the carrots and broccoli. Using a spiralizer to make zucchini into spaghetti type noodles. Cut them into short strips.

Place celery, carrots, broccoli, zucchini and corn in a bowl and cover with the blended soup base. Add salt and pepper if desired.

Mexican Vegetable Soup

Ingredients

- 2 c. vegetable base (page 25)

Vegetables

- 1 tbsp. cold pressed olive oil
- ½ yellow or orange bell pepper, diced
- 1 red bell pepper, diced
- 1 tbsp. cumin seeds, ground
- ½ tsp. dried oregano
- ¼ tsp. cayenne pepper
- 1 tomatoes, diced
- 1 tbsp. jalapeno pepper, diced
- 1 c. corn kernels
- 1 zucchini, diced
- himalayan crystal salt or natural sea salt to taste
- pepper to taste

Optional Toppings

- lime juice
- avocado
- cilantro
- sour cream

Directions

Make vegetable base and set aside.

In bowl, place olive oil, bell peppers, red onion, jalapeno, zucchini, corn, salt, and spices.

Pour the vegetable base over the mixture and stir. May warm in dehydrator for about 1-3 hours.

Add the tomatoes and any optional toppings. Serve immediately with optional toppings.

Mexican Vegetable Soup

Makes 4-8 Servings

Preparation Time:
30
Minutes

Drying Time:
1 - 3
Hours

I am a fan of Mexican flavors and vegetable soup is a good way to get that taste with lower fat.

Watermelon Soup

Makes 6-8 Servings

Preparation Time:
20
Minutes

Cill Time:
60
Minutes

Watermelon soup is a good summer soup. Like most fruit soups, it's served cold during warm weather.

Watermelon Soup

Ingredients

- 5 c. watermelon, cut and seeded
- 1 ½ c. raw cashews
- 3 zucchinis, cut into pieces
- ¼ c. raw liquid sweetener
- 2 tbsp. mint, chopped finely
- 1 pint berries (strawberries, blackberries)
- water if needed

Directions

Puree the watermelon in a blender. This may need to be done in batches. Pour the watermelon puree in a bowl and set aside.

In a blender, mix the cashews, raw liquid sweetener and one tablespoon of mint until it is creamy. Add water, as needed. It should look like a thick cream.

Place the berries in the bowl with the watermelon, add the cashew mixture, and gently mix. Add remaining mint and garnish with a whole mint leaf.

Fun Fact:

Watermelon flesh is not just pink/red but also comes in yellow. The yellow watermelon is part of the Citrullus lanatus family. It is yellow because it does not have lycopene. The yellow flesh may have more of a honey flavor.

Gazpacho

Preparation: 25 Min.
Makes 6-8 Servings

Ingredients

- 6 large tomatoes, chopped
- 2 tbsp. lemon juice
- 2 cloves garlic
- 1 large zucchini, chopped
- 4 green onions, chopped
- 2 red bell pepper, chopped
- Himalayan crystal salt or sea salt to taste

Directions

Juice the lemon and place the juice in a blender with the garlic, salt, zucchini, tomatoes and green onion.

Mix until you have a nice smooth soup base, adding pure water to achieve the desired constancy.

Chop reaming three (3) tomatoes and bell peppers and place in a bowl. Pour the base over chopped vegetables and serve.

Fun Fact:

Gazpacho is a soup made of raw vegetables and served cold. There are many theories about the origin of this soup but all agree that it has ancient roots.

The internationally known red gazpacho with tomatoes evolved in the 19th century. However, today it can very with different colors and ingredients.

It is a refreshing meal eaten during the hot summer and very popular in Spain and Portugal.

Fresh Garden Soup

Preparation: 30 Min. *Makes 4-6 Servings*

Ingredients

- 3 green onions, chopped
- 1 c. turnip, diced
- 1 c. carrots, thinly sliced
- 1 c. celery, thinly sliced
- 1 c. zucchini, chopped
- 1 c. summer yellow squash, chopped
- 1 c. cabbage, shredded
- 4 c. tomatoes
- ½ tsp. Himalayan crystal salt or sea salt
- ½ tsp. black pepper
- ½ tsp. basil
- ½ tsp. oregano
- ½ tsp. rosemary
- 2 cloves garlic, pressed
- 2 tsp. cold pressed olive oil

Directions

Chop green onion, turnip, zucchini, and yellow squash and place them in a bowl. Shred the cabbage and thinly slice the carrots and celery. Place them in the bowl and toss.

Place tomatoes in a blender. Add the salt, pepper, basil, oregano, rosemary, garlic, and olive oil then blend until well mixed.

Pour tomato mixture over the vegetables. You may warm to 100° F, if desired.

Fun Fact:

In traditional French cuisine, soups are classified into two main groups: clear soups and thick soups.

Italian Tomato Soup

Preparation: 20 Min. *Makes 4-6 Servings*

Ingredients

- 1 c. dried tomatoes
- 6 fresh tomatoes
- ½ tbsp. Italian seasoning
- 2-3 green onions
- 1-2 zucchinis
- 2-4 cloves garlic
- 3 tbsp. cold pressed olive oil (optional)
- Himalayan crystal salt or sea salt to taste
- pepper to taste
- sunflower greens, for garnish

Directions

Soak dried tomatoes in water for 15 minutes and place in a blender.

Add fresh tomatoes, green onions, zucchini, yellow squash, garlic, olive oil, salt and pepper and blend until smooth.

Place in soup bowls and garnish with sunflower greens.

Fun Fact:

Sunflower greens are part of a group of greens called micro-greens. Sunflower greens are the green part of the sprouted sunflower seeds grown for about seven days.

Vegetable Base

Preparation: 10 Min. Makes 4-6 Servings

Ingredients

- ½ c. onion
- 1 c. turnip
- 1 c. parsnip
- 8 c. celery
- 1 c. zucchini, diced
- Himalayan crystal salt or natural sea salt to taste
- pepper to taste

Directions

Combine onion, carrots, turnip, zucchini, parsnip, and celery in a blender.

Pour mixture into mylk bag or a clean nylon knee high and strain over a bowl. Squeeze to ensure all liquid is removed.

Add spices to the juice and let set for at least an hour.

Note

The leftover vegetable pulp makes a good start for raw crackers. Just add soaked nuts and or seeds, seasoning and any other vegetables, then dry in dehydrator.

Fun Fact:

The key to making soups is to have a great base. Something that can be made into any flavor pallet. Soup base is the culmination of layering of flavors.

"Pasta" Primavera

Preparation: 20 Min. *Makes 6-8 Servings*

Ingredients

- 1 tomato chopped
- ½ yellow bell pepper, thinly sliced
- ½ red bell pepper, thinly sliced
- 2 c. broccoli florets
- 1 large carrot shredded
- 3 c. zucchini shredded to look like spaghetti
- 1 clove garlic pressed
- ½ c. ricotta cheese sauce (page 105)
- 2 tbsp. lemon juiced
- Himalayan crystal salt or sea salt to taste
- pepper to taste

Directions

To ½ cup ricotta cheese sauce, recipe in this book, add lemon juice, salt and pepper to taste.

Use a spiral slicer or shred zucchini to look like spaghetti and place in a bowl.

Wash and prepare broccoli, carrots, red and yellow bell pepper, tomatoes and garlic then place in the bowl with zucchini.

Gently mix the ricotta cheese sauce with the vegetables. Flavor with salt and pepper.

Fun Fact:

Primavera is spring in Italian. In the culinary world, primavera is the adding of fresh vegetables during its preparation. Pasta primavera is a pasta dish with a multitude of vegetables and may or may not have a cream sauce

Apple Zucchini Salad

Preparation: 15 Min. *Makes 6-8 Servings*

Ingredients

Dressing

- 1 tbsp. cold pressed olive oil
- 1 tbsp. lemon, juiced
- 1 lime, juiced
- 1 tsp. nutmeg
- 1 tsp. basil
- ¼ tsp. pepper

Salad

- 3 medium apples, cored and diced
- ½ medium red onion, thinly sliced lengthwise
- 1 red bell pepper, sliced into matchsticks
- 1 pound zucchini, sliced thinly

Directions

To make the dressing, juice the lime and lemon and place the juice in a large salad bowl. Then add the oil, nutmeg, basil and pepper and mix.

Cut and core apples and place in the same bowl with the dressing and coat them well.

Cut and prepare onion, bell pepper and zucchini then place in the bowl with the apples and dressing and gently toss. Serve and in enjoy.

Fun Fact:

The crabapple is the only apple native of North America even though there are 2,500 **apple** varieties grown in United States.

Vegetable Ribbion Salad

Ingredients

Salad

- 1 c. carrots, thinly sliced
- 1 c. zucchini, zooodles
- ½ c. beet, zoodled
- 2 c. cabbage, thinly sliced
- 1 avocado, thinly sliced

Dressing

- 1 clove garlic
- ¼ c. basil, fresh
- 4 tbsp. parsley
- ½ lemon, juiced
- Salt and pepper to taste

Directions

Use a spiralizer to make the thin strips of zucchini and beets. Thinly slice carrots with a knife, vegetable peeler or mandolin lengthwise.

Shred cabbage using a mandolin or knife. Place in a bowl then add zucchini, carrots and beets. Toss with the dressing just before serving.

Thinly slice the avocado and layer over top of the salad.

To make the dressing, combine garlic, basil, leek, parsley, salt, pepper and lemon juice in a blender.

Vegetable Ribbion Salad

Makes 4-6 Servings

Preparation Time:
10
Minutes

This easy salad gets its name from
the colorful ribbons of vegetables noodles.

"Tuna" Salad

Makes 6-8 Servings

Preparation Time:
15
Minutes

Soaking Time:
8-12
Hours

The zucchini gives this "tuna" recipe a nice
creamy texture. There is no need to add extra mayo.

"Tuna" Salad

Ingredients

"Tuna"

- 1 c. sunflower seeds, soaked overnight
- ¼ c. onion, minced
- Himalayan crystal salt or natural sea to taste
- 1 lemon, juiced
- 2 stocks of celery
- 1 tbsp. kelp
- 1 zucchini

Salad

- 2 c. lettuce
- ½ c. radishes
- ¼ c. celery
- 1 avocado, sliced
- 2 tomatoes, sliced

Directions

Soak sunflower seeds overnight. Drain water and rinse seeds then place in a food processor.

Cut celery into half inch pieces and add celery, onion, salt, lemon juice, zucchini and kelp in the food processor. Blend until roughly mixed.

Wash and tear lettuce into bite size pieces on a plate. Scoop about ½ cup of "tuna" into the center of the lettuce. Place radishes and tomatoes around "tuna." May use sliced avocado. Garnish with sliced celery on top of "tuna."

Variation

To make a **tuna wrap**, take the romaine leaf lettuce and place the tuna mixture down the spine. On top of that add your sliced tomato and avocado. Roll the lettuce leaf and enjoy.

Moroccan Buckwheat Salad

Ingredients

- 1 c. buckwheat groats, soaked
- handful kale
- ½ c. carrots
- 1 avocado
- 1 lemon, juiced
- 1 c. zucchini, chopped
- ½ c. cashews (optional)
- 1 tsp. cinnamon
- 1 tsp. allspice
- ¼ c. fresh mint, chopped
- ½ tsp. Himalayan crystal salt
- pepper to taste
- 1 tsp. cold pressed olive oil

Directions

Soak buckwheat overnight. Drain off water and rinse, then place into a bowl.

Wash kale remove steam and tear into small pieces and add to the bowl with buckwheat.

Chop mint, shred carrots, slice zucchini and cube avocados then toss in with buckwheat and kale mixture. Add cashews and mix.

Juice lemon in a small bowl. To lemon juice, add olive oil, cinnamon, allspice, salt and pepper mix and pour over vegetables and toss.

Fun Fact:

Kale has an old history. It was popular in Europe during roman time and the middle ages.

Moroccan Buckwheat Salad

Makes 2-4 Servings

Preparation Time:
25
Minutes

Soaking Time:
8-12
Hours

Despite its name, buckwheat does not belong to the wheat family. In fact, buckwheat is related to sorrel and rhubarb. And is safe to eat on a gluten free diet because there is not gluten in buckwheat.

Almond Delight

Makes 4-6 Servings

Preparation Time:
30
Minutes

Soaking Time:
4-8
Hours

Almonds were prized ingredient in breads served and consumed by Egyptian pharos.

Almond Delight

Ingredients

Pepper Sauce

- 1 c. almonds, soaked overnight and peeled
- 1 red bell peppers
- ½ tsp. dried thyme
- ½ tsp. dried tarragon
- ½ tsp. dried marjoram
- pinch paprika
- ¼ tsp. Himalayan crystal salt or sea salt
- ¼ c. pure water (more or less as needed)

"Pasta"

- 3-4 small zucchinis, shredded to look like "spaghetti"
- 1 c. broccoli cut in small, bite-sized pieces
- ½ c. asparagus, shredded
- 3 large yellow or red bell peppers, cut in long slivers
- 2 c. spinach, chopped coarsely
- ½ c. fresh basil, finely chopped
- 2 tsp. poppy seeds
- Himalayan crystal salt or sea salt to taste
- pepper to taste
- 1 tomato, sliced for garnish

Directions

Soak almonds overnight. Peel the brown skin off the almonds and drain the water.

Mix almonds, bell pepper, thyme, tarragon, marjoram, paprika and salt. and water in a blender until smooth and creamy. (More or less water may be needed.)

Prepare zucchini, broccoli, asparagus, bell pepper, spinach, basil, poppy seeds, salt and pepper then place them in a bowl.

Gently toss together Pepper Sauce with the vegetable "pasta." Garnish with sun-dried tomatoes.

Snappy Vegetables

Ingredients

- 2 c. sugar snap peas
- 1 red bell pepper
- 1 zucchini squash
- 1 cloves garlic, minced
- 1 lemon, juiced
- 1 tbsp. Italian seasoning
- 1 head lettuce
- ½ c. macadamia nuts or cashews, grated

Directions

Wash and prepare all vegetables. Make sure to remove strings from snap peas. Slice the bell pepper and zucchini and place in a bowl.

In a separate bowl or jar with a lid, combine lemon oil, Italian seasoning, and garlic. After mixing the dressing pour over the vegetables and toss together.

Line a serving plate with the lettuce, then place the vegetables over the greens. Use the grated macadamia nuts as "cheese" and sprinkle over top.

Fun Fact:

Except for in stores that sell specialized foreign foods, **Italian Seasoning** does not exist in Italy. Italian cooks prefer to use one or two herbs in their cooking. Therefore, there is no real seasoning blend that compares to this American made blend. We have it because these herbs, (rosemary, basil, oregano, sage, marjoram, etc.), remind us of the flavors we have come to associate with Italy.

Snappy Vegetables

Makes 2-4 Servings

Preparation Time:
   15
   Minutes

Sugar snap peas are a cross between English and Snow Peas. They became commonly available in the 1970s. Today they are commonly consider finger food.

Flora's Albanian Salad

Makes 2-4 Servings

Preparation Time:
10
Minutes

My friend Flora a native of Albania gave me this recipe. She said that when she was growing up that this was a common salad to eat.

Flora's Albanian Salad

Ingredients

- 2 cucumbers, thinly sliced
- 1 zucchini, thinly sliced
- 2 tomatoes, sliced
- ½ red bell pepper, sliced
- ½ orange, or yellow bell pepper, sliced
- 2 tsp. cold pressed olive oil
- 2 tbsp. lemon, juiced
- Himalayan crystal salt or natural sea salt to taste
- black pepper to taste

Directions

Prepare vegetables and set aside.

In a small jar with a lid, place the oil, lemon juice, salt, and pepper. Secure the jar lid then and shake it until well mixed.

Pour dressing over vegetables and toss. Arrange on a plate and serve.

Fun Fact:

Cool as a *cucmber* is not just a saying about people but the fact that cucumbers are 20 degrees cooler inside than they are outside.

Not only are they a cool vegetable but they contain many vitamins needed daily including Vitamin B1, Vitamin B2, Vitamin B3, Vitamin B5, Vitamin B6, Folic Acid, Vitamin C, Calcium, Iron, Magnesium, Phosphorus, Potassium and Zinc.

With all the B Vitamins, cucumbers may provide a quick pick-me-up.

Green Zoodles

Ingredients

Pesto

- ½ c. fresh spinach leaves
- ¼ c. fresh parsley
- 1 tbsp. dried basil
- 1 tbsp. dried oregano
- 1-3 cloves garlic, minced
- 1-2 green onion
- ½ c. pumpkin seeds, soaked 3-5 hours
- ½ small zucchini, shredded
- 2 or more tbsp. cold pressed olive oil
- Himalayan crystal salt or sea salt to taste
- pure water as needed

Zoodles

- 3-6 small zucchinis, spiraled or shredded (like spaghetti)

Directions

Soak the pumpkin seeds in water that covers them at least 3 hours. They can be soaked overnight if desired.

Make pesto by placing spinach, parsley, garlic, onion, zucchini, pumpkin seeds, oil and spices in a food processor or blender. Puree to semi-smooth paste. Add water as needed.

Use a spiral slicer or shred zucchini to look like spaghetti. Place on a plate and pour pesto over top. If desired garnish with pumpkin seeds or tomatoes.

Fun Fact:

Pesto orientated in Genoa, Italy in the 16th century.

Green Zoodles

Makes 4-6 Servings

Preparation Time:
20
Minutes

Soaking Time:
3-5
Hours

Zucchini cut using a spiralizer are known as zoodles. Zoodles are a healthy and gluten-free alternative to pasta.

Zucchini Mexicali

Makes 4-6 Servings

Preparation Time:
 30
 Minutes

Zucchini Mexicali is a tasty and easy dish to make.
This recipe is a big hit at potlucks.

Zucchini Mexicali

Ingredients

Vegetables

- 3 c. zucchinis, sliced
- 1 large carrot, sliced
- ¾ c. celery, chopped
- 1 ½ small tomatoes, chopped

Mexicali Sauce

- ½ small onion, chopped
- 1-2 cloves garlic, chopped
- basil, to taste, chopped
- ground coriander, to taste
- Mexican seasoning, to taste
- juice of one lime
- 1 jalapeno pepper, chopped
- 2-3 medium tomatoes, chopped

Directions

Blend the lime juice in a blender with the onion, garlic, basil, coriander, Mexican seasoning, jalapeno and tomatoes and mix until smooth.

Thinly slice zucchini and carrots and place in a bowl. Chop celery and 2-4 tomatoes and mix into the bowl with zucchini and carrots.

Pour the Mexicali sauce over the vegetables.

Serve as a salad or wrap in a lettuce or cabbage leaf for more of a "burrito" feel.

Tomatoes and Zucchinis

Preparation: 20 Min. *Makes 6-8 Servings*

Ingredients

- 3 c. zucchinis, sliced
- ½ onion, chopped
- 1 clove garlic, minced
- 2 tbsp. Italian seasoning
- 2-4 tomatoes
- Himalayan salt or sea salt to taste
- pepper to taste

Directions

Place 2 ½ cups of zucchini in a serving dish, salt and pepper to taste and set aside.

In a blender, mix remaining ½ cup of zucchini, onion, garlic and seasonings until creamy.

Pour over zucchini and top with sliced tomatoes.

May top with macadamia nuts or Spicy Nut Cheese (page 112) as a garnish.

Fun Fact:

Tomatoes are technically a fruit but the government wanted to tax them, so tomatoes was classified a vegetable in the 1800's

The Universities of Manchester and Newcastle, England, have research indicating that tomatoes may be acting as a kind of internal sunscreen by blocking UV rays.

Zoodle Salad

Preparation: 15 Min. *Makes 4-6 Servings*

Ingredients

Sauce

- ¼ c. dried tomatoes
- 1 tbsp. cold pressed olive oil
- ¼ c. avocado
- 3 tbsp. lemon, juiced

Salad

- 3 c. tomatoes, chopped
- 2 cucumbers, sliced
- 2 small zucchinis, shredded

Directions

Soak dried tomatoes in enough pure water to cover for about 10 minutes. Remove the tomatoes and place in a blender. Reserve soaking water from tomatoes for later use.

To the tomatoes add olive oil, avocado and lemon juice and mix until well blended. Add tomato soaking water until a creamy textured is achieved.

Chop fresh tomatoes, slice cumberers and zoodle zucchini, and then, place in a bowl. Pour sauce over salad and toss.

Green Dressing

Preparation: 15 Min. *Makes 4-6 Servings*

Ingredients

- 1 c. nut mayo (page 109)
- 1 large avocado
- 1 c. spinach
- 1 lime, juiced
- 1 small cucumber
- 1 small zucchini
- enough pure water to blend

Directions

Wash and roughly cut the ingredients and place in a blender. Blend until smooth.

Z Spinach Salad

Preparation: 20 Min. *Makes* 4-6 Servings

Ingredients

Salad

- 3 c. mixed baby lettuce and spinach
- 1 c. zucchini, cubed
- ½ c. strawberries, halved
- ½ c. walnuts, soaked and then dried
- ¼ c. small red onion, thinly sliced

Strawberry Dressing

- ½ c. fresh strawberries
- 1 tbsp. lime juice
- 2 tbsp. coconut nectar
- ½ c. zucchini
- 1 tsp. poppy seeds
- Himalayan crystal salt or sea salt to taste
- white pepper to taste

Directions

To make the dressing, place strawberries in a juicer.

Combine strawberry juice, lime juice, coconut nectar, zucchini, poppy seeds, salt and pepper in a blender and mix well.

While blender is running, slowly add the water until the desired texture is achieved.

Wash baby lettuces and spinach, cut zucchini, strawberries and onion with soaked and dried walnuts.

Add dressing to salad just before serving.

Zucchini Vinaigrette

In a blender, place marinade and reserved vegetables, from zucchini marinated vegetables (page 47).

And one more chopped zucchini. Blend the ingredients until smooth and creamy.

Zucchini Marinated Vegetables

Preparation: 30 Min.   *Marinating: 1-3 Days*   *Makes 4-6 Servings*

Ingredients

Marinade

- 2 tbsp. cold pressed olive oil
- 1 lemon, juiced
- 2 tsp. raw apple cider vinegar
- 1 clove garlic
- 2 tsp. Italian seasoning
- 1 tsp. basil
- ½ tsp. Himalayan crystal salt

Vegetables

- 1 c. cauliflower, chopped
- 2 carrots, sliced
- ½ - 1 c. onion, chopped
- 1 jalapeno pepper, chopped
- 2 c. zucchini, chopped
- ½ yellow bell pepper, chopped
- ½ red bell pepper, chopped

Directions

Chop cauliflower, onion, zucchini, jalapeno pepper and bell peppers then place in a bowl.

Note: if you like hot food include the whole jalapeno seeds included.

Wash and slice carrots and then place in a bowl with the cauliflower and mix.

In a blender place the olive oil, lemon juice, raw apple cider vinegar, garlic, Italian seasoning, basil and salt. Pour over the cut vegetables and marinate for 1-3 days.

Reserve ½ cup of the vegetables and marinade for Zucchini Vinaigrette.

Remove remaining vegetable from the marinade and enjoy.

Buttered Zucchini

Ingredients

Butter Sauce

- ¼ tsp. turmeric
- ½ tsp. himalayan crystal salt or sea salt
- ¼ c. cold pressed olive oil, more as desired

Noodles

- 4 c. zucchini or other squash, shredded
- ¼ c. onion, chopped
- ¼ c. sunflower seeds, soaked and dried
- ¼ c. pumpkin seeds, soaked and dried
- 1 tbsp. dried basil
- ½ tsp. black pepper

Directions

Use a spiral slicer or shred the zucchini for zoodles and place in a large bowl.

Then add onion, sunflower, pumpkin seeds, basil and black pepper to the zucchini and gently toss together.

In a small bowl mix oil, turmeric and salt in a small bowl and mix.

Pour the butter sauce over zucchini noodles and gently.

Fun Fact:

Zoodles are made with a spiral slicer, julienne peeler or even a vegetable peeler. The result is long curly 'noodles.'

Side & Main Dishes

Quiche with Tomato

Jalapeno Zucchini Fritters

Makes 2-4 Servings

Preparation Time: **20** Minutes
Soaking Time: **2-12** Hours
Drying Time: **5-8** Hours

Fritters are traditionally a fried pastry usually consisting of a portion of batter or breading which has been filled with bits of meat, seafood, fruit, vegetables or other ingredients. This fritter is a savory version that is nut and oil free. I could say it is "air fried"

Jalapeno Zucchini Fritters

Ingredients

Fritters

- 3-4 medium size zucchini, grated
- 2 jalapeno, diced
- 2 sprigs of parsley
- 2 green onions, chopped
- 1 tsp. paprika
- 1 tbsp. cumin, ground
- 1 tbsp. chili powder
- 2 tbsp. onion, chopped
- 1 clove garlic
- 1 tbsp. nutritional yeast (optional)
- 2 cloves, garlic, minced
- 3 tbsp. Irish moss gel
- ¼ c. coconut flour
- 1 tsp. Himalayan crystal salt
- 1 tbsp. lime juice
- 1 tsp. lime zest

Avocado Cream

- ½ c. almond sour cream
- 1 avocado
- ½ c. romaine lettuce, chopped
- ¼ c. parsley
- 1 lime, juiced
- lime zest
- 1 tsp. Himalayan crystal salt

Directions

In a bowl with a cheese cloth grate zucchini, sprinkle with salt and let stand for 10 minutes. Take a cheese cloth or mesh nut mylk bag and place zucchini in it and squeeze out excess water.

In a food processor, combine jalapeno, parsley, onions, paprika, cumin, chili powder, Irish moss gel, nutritional yeast, garlic, salt lime juice and lime zest. Until reaching a semi-thick consistency. If too thin, add coconut flour.

Place the mixture in a bowl and add zucchini and mix by hand. The consistency should be thick not soupy.

Form zucchini mixture into a patty, about ¼ to ½ inch thick, the thicker patties take longer to dry.

Dry in dehydrator on a nonstick sheet for about 5 hours, flip ½ way and remove the nonstick dehydrator sheet.

Avocado Cream:

In a food processor, combine the lettuce, parsley, avocado, salt and almond sour cream until well mixed. Place in refrigerator until ready to serve. Top patties with avocado cream, cilantro, and serve immediately.

Cabbage Roll

Preparation: 20 Min. *Soaking:* 1 Hr. *Makes 4-6 Servings*

Ingredients

- 4 cabbage leaves
- 1 c. sprouted quinoa
- 2 tbsp. onion
- ½ c. zucchini
- ½ c. celery
- 2 tbsp. parsley
- 1 tsp. paprika
- 1 tsp. basil
- ½ tsp. marjoram
- ½ tsp. thyme
- ½ tsp. black pepper

Directions

Place onion, zucchini, celery parsley, paprika, basil, marjoram, thyme, and pepper in a food processor and mix until consistent sizes. Place in a bowl and add quinoa and mix.

Peel and wash four large cabbage leaves. Place quinoa mixture in the leaves and roll. Use a tooth pick to close, if needed.

Place cabbage rolls seam side down In a baking pan. Dry about 2-4 hours, if desired.

Parsnip Rice

Ingredients

- 3 medium parsnips
- 1 clove garlic
- 2 tbsp. onion, chopped
- 2 tbsp. lemon, juiced
- ¼ tsp. Himalayan crystal salt
- ½ tsp. black pepper

Directions

Peel the parsnips and cut off the tops and bottoms. Coarsely chop the parsnips and then pulse in the food processor until it looks like rice. Add the onion, lemon, garlic, salt and pepper pulse a few times until rice is well mixed.

Stroganoff

Preparation: 25 Min. *Makes 4-6 Servings*

Ingredients

- ¼ c. brown mushrooms
- ½ c. cashews, soaked 2-4 hours
- ¼ tsp. Himalayan crystal salt or sea salt
- 1 tbsp. lemon, juiced
- 1 tsp. cold pressed olive oil
- 1 tbsp. nut/seed mylk (page 110)
- 2 tbsp. tahini
- 1 tbsp. poultry seasoning
- ¼ c. onion
- ¼ tsp. paprika
- ½ tsp. thyme, dried
- 1 tbsp. dill, dried
- freshly ground pepper to taste
- pure water
- 4-5 medium zucchinis, shredded

Directions

Shred or spiralize zucchini into noodles and set aside.

In a blender, combine mushrooms, cashews, lemon juice, olive oil, nut cheese, tahini, onion, and seasoning. As the blender is combining the ingredients, add only enough water to make a creamy consistency.

On a plate, place noodles, and cover with stroganoff mixture from your blender. Enjoy.

Variations

1) Instead of using zucchini noodles, sprout 1 cup wild rice and place stroganoff mixture on top of sprouted rice.

2) Use parsnip rice in place of zoodles and place stroganoff on top of parsnip rice.

Cravin' Mac & Cheese

Ingredients

Sauce

- ½ c. cashews
- ¼ c. pumpkin seeds
- 1 lemon, juiced
- ½ orange, juiced
- ¾ tsp. Himalayan crystal salt
- 1-2 cloves garlic
- 1 tsp. mustard powder
- ½ tsp. turmeric powder or fresh

Noodles

- 1 c. butternut squash, peeled & shredded
- 1 c. zucchini, peeled and shredded

'Bread' Topping

- ¼ c. walnuts soaked
- ¼ tsp. Himalayan crystal salt
- ¼ tsp. thyme
- ¼ tsp. rosemary
- ½ tsp. basil

Directions

Soak pumpkin seeds overnight, drain them, and set aside.

In a blender, combine cashews, pumpkin seeds, lemon, orange juice, garlic, mustard powder, salt and turmeric until creamy. Use only enough water to make it a nice creamy consistency.

Use very ripe butternut, the riper it is the easier they are to shred and eat. Cut and shred the butternut and zucchini squash. Place the shredded squash along with creamy sauce and mix it with the noodles.

In a food processor mix dry walnuts, thyme, rosemary and basil until looks like bread crumbs. Sprinkle over the top of the noodles.

May put in dehydrator at 100°F until warm if desired.

Cravin' Mac & Cheese

Makes 2-4 Servings

Preparation Time: 20 Minutes

Soaking Time: 2-12 Hours

Drying Time: 5-8 Hours

I made this dish when I was cravin' mac and cheese. I had a refrigerator full of leftovers and put them together. This dish satisfies that craving.

Vegetables with Creamy Mustard

Makes 4-6 Servings

Preparation Time:
 20
Minutes

French monks mixed ground mustard seeds with "must," an unfermented wine which inspired the word "mustard"

Vegetables with Creamy Mustard

Ingredients

Vegetables

- 2-4 cloves garlic, minced
- 2 large red bell peppers, chopped
- 1 c. zucchini, thinly sliced
- 1 tbsp. green onions, finely chopped
- 1 small carrot thinly slice
- 1 stick celery, thinly slice
- lettuce, for garnish
- tomatoes, for garnish

Sauce

- ½ c. cashews
- ½ lemon, juiced
- 1 tbsp. mustard powder
- ½ tsp. cold pressed olive oil
- ½ c. water
- ½ tsp. Himalayan crystal salt

Directions

Slice zucchini, carrot and celery. Chop garlic, bell pepper, and green onion and place vegetables in a bowl, then set aside.

In a blender, mix cashews, lemon juice, mustard powder, cold pressed olive oil and salt, adding water as needed to make it creamy.

Pour the sauce over the vegetables and toss. Let the flavors mingle for an hour for improved flavor.

Serve over lettuce and tomatoes.

Zucchini Casserole

Preparation: 20 Min. *Makes 4-6 Servings*

Ingredients

- ¼ c. walnuts, chopped

Dressing

- 1 lemon, juiced
- ½ tsp. basil
- ½ tsp. oregano
- 2 cloves garlic, pressed
- Himalayan crystal salt or sea salt to taste
- pepper to taste

Vegetables

- ¼ c. mushrooms, slivered
- ¼ c. onion, chopped
- ½ c. red bell pepper, chopped
- ½ c. broccoli, chopped
- ½ c. carrot, shredded
- ½ c. tomatoes, chopped
- ¼ c. fresh parsley, chopped
- 1 c. zucchini, shredded

Directions

Juice lemon and place juice in a bowl. Add basil, oregano, garlic, salt and pepper then mix and set aside.

Slice mushrooms, grate zucchini and carrots. Chop parsley, broccoli, tomatoes, bell pepper and onion then place in a casserole pan.

Pour dressing over the vegetables and toss. Top with grated walnuts.

Fun Fact:

Black pepper is the fruit of a flowering vine that is dried. Black pepper is native to south India.

Zucchini Casserole

Makes 4-6 Servings

Preparation Time:
15
Minutes

Drying Time:
4-8
Hours

The word casserole originally referred to the pan in which the dish was cooked. While this recipe is not cooked in a casserole pan it can be served in one and has the comfort feel of one.

Dragon Eggs

Makes 6-8 Servings

Preparation Time: **40** Minutes
Soaking Time: **1-12** Hours
Drying Time: **5-8** Hours

Dagon eggs are very rare and it takes a knight in shining armor to bring them home to loved ones. Seriously dragon eggs are my answer to eggrolls.

Dragon Eggs

Ingredients

Filling

- 1 tsp. fresh ginger
- 2 ½ tsp. coriander
- 2 scallions
- 1 c. bean sprouts
- 1 c. red cabbage, sliced thinly
- 1 zucchini, thinly sliced
- 1 c. broccoli, chopped
- 2-4 stocks celery, finely chopped
- 1 inch lemon, grass, soaked and chopped
- 1 tbsp. Himalayan chrystal salt or natural sea salt
- 1 tsp. black pepper

Dragon Dressing

- ¼ c. lemon, juiced
- 2 tbsp. cold pressed olive oil or cold pressed sesame oil
- 1 tbsp. tarragon leaves
- 1 tsp. mustard powder
- pinch cayenne

Skin

- 2 tsp. Himalayan chrystal salt or natural sea salt
- ½ c. onion
- 3-4 stocks of celery
- 2-3 cloves garlic
- 3 c. sesame pulp, left over after making sesame mylk
- 1 ½ c. gold flax, ground in coffee grinder

Dragon Dipping Sauce

- 1 cucumber, chopped
- 1 zucchini, chopped
- 2 stocks celery, cut into half-inch pieces
- ¼ c. walnuts, soaked
- 1 tsp. cold pressed sesame oil or flax oil
- 1 ½ tsp. Himalayan chrystal salt or natural sea salt
- 2 tsp. black pepper
- 1 tsp. hot curry powder
- 2 tsp. raw apple cider vinegar

Directions on the next page...

...Dragon Eggs continued

Directions

In a bowl combine ginger, coriander, scallions, bean sprouts, red cabbage, broccoli, zucchini, celery, lemongrass, salt and pepper. Gently toss and set aside.

In a small jar combine lemon juice, cold pressed sesame oil, tarragon leaves, mustard powder, and cayenne. Place lid on jar and mix well.

Pour dressing over the prepared vegetables and gently toss. Set aside to marinate, while making the skin.

In a food processor, place sesame pulp, ground flaxseed, garlic, celery, onion and salt. Combine until well blended.

Once skin ingredients are mixed, divide into 2 equal parts. Spread each part out on parchment paper. With rolling pin roll out each side. Both parts should be of equal size. Use extra piece of parchment paper on the top so it will be easier to peel and not stick to your rolling pin.

On one piece of the skin spoon prepared vegetables with dressing. Place the remaining skin over top of filling and pinch the edges together so the filling stays in place.

Cut dragon eggs into 2 inch pieces. Place in a dehydrator for about 5 to 8 hours at about 100°F.

While dragon eggs are, drying prepare Dragon Dipping Sauce. In a blender combine cucumber, zucchini, celery cut into half-inch pieces, walnuts, oil, salt and pepper, curry powder, and raw apple cider vinegar. Blend until well combined and serve with Dragon eggs.

Cardamom Rice

Preparation: 20 Min.　　Soaking: 8-12 Hr.　　Makes 4-6 Servings

Ingredients

Vegetables

- ¼ c. green beans, chopped
- ¼ c. cauliflower, chopped
- ¼ c. zucchini, chopped
- ¼ c. broccoli, chopped
- 1-2 cloves garlic, minced
- 1 onion, diced

Rice

- 3 c. wild rice, sprouted
- 1 tbsp. cardamom seeds, soaked overnight

Sauce

- 5 red bell peppers
- 1 tsp. cold pressed olive oil
- 3 tbsp. water
- 1 tsp. curry powder
- 1-2 tsp. turmeric powder

Directions

Sprout rice (see page 122). In a separate bowl soak cardamom seeds overnight. Combine rice with cardamom and set aside.

Clean and chop green beans, cauliflower, zucchini, broccoli, onion, and garlic then mix and set aside.

Seed and dice peppers and place in a blender. Blend the oil, curry powder, turmeric and water until smooth.

Arrange on a serving plate with rice on the bottom, then scoop vegetables on top. Pour sauce over the vegetables and enjoy.

Zucchini Boat

Ingredients

Vegetables

- 4 zucchinis, shredded
- 1 green onion, chopped
- 1 tomato, chopped
- ½ tsp. Himalayan crystal salt
- ¼ tsp. pepper
- ½ red, yellow or orange bell pepper, chopped
- ½ c. snow pea pods
- 1 clove garlic

Sauce

- lemon, zest
- ½ lemon, juiced
- ¼ c. mayo (page 109)
- 2 tsp mustard seed, ground

Directions

In a small bowl, mix mayo, lemon juice, lemon zest, ground mustard seed, salt and pepper. Set it aside.

Slice 2 zucchinis lengthwise in half. Scoop out the middle leaving enough on the sides to make a boat or zucchini bowl. Set aside. Shred remaining zucchini and place in a bowl.

Wash and chop green onion, bell pepper, tomato and garlic then add to the zucchini. Wash pea pods and add them to the bowl.

Pour sauce over the vegetables and mix. Take zucchini mixture and spoon inside zucchini halves then place on the dehydrator with nonstick sheet. Dry at 100° for about 2 hours.

Zucchini Boat

Makes 4-6 Servings

Preparation Time:
45
Minutes

Drying Time:
1-3
Hours

Zucchini boats are hollowed out zucchini
which is filled with creamy sauce and vegetables.

Lasagna

Makes 4-6 Servings

Preparation Time:
45
Minutes

Soaking Time:
30
Minutes

Drying Time:
60
Minutes

Lasagna is a family favorite. When I transitioned to raw foods I missed the cheesy vegetable lasagna and the raw food versions were not satisfying that need. So, I created this decadent raw version.

Lasagna

Ingredients

- pumpkin seeds, optional

Zoodles

- 3 large zucchini

Meatless

- 2 c. walnuts, soaked
- 1 tsp. poultry seasoning
- 1 tsp. italian seasoning
- 1 clove garlic
- 4 tbsp. onion
- ½ tsp. Himalayan crystal salt or sea salt

Veggies

- 1 ½ c. spinach, cleaned and stems removed
- 1 colored bell pepper, chopped
- any other vegetables you choose

Cheese Sauce

- 2 c. cashews
- 1 clove garlic
- 1 tsp. Italian seasoning
- ½ tsp. Himalayan crystal salt
- 4 tbsp. cold pressed olive oil
- 1 c. pure water or more as needed

Marinara Sauce

- 1 c. dried tomatoes
- ¼ c. cold pressed olive oil
- 2-3 tomatoes
- 1 tsp. basil
- 1 tsp. oregano
- 1 tsp. Himalayan crystal salt
- 2-3 cloves garlic
- ¼ c. onion

Directions

Pumpkin Seeds

Soak and dry the seeds (page 122). Roughly chop seeds and set aside.

Zoodles

Using a mandolin, slice the zucchini into thin slices. Lay flat on dehydrator tray. Dry at 100° for about 30 minutes. These become zoodles (or noodles.)

Meatless

Soak walnuts, in enough water to cover, overnight.

Directions on the next page...

...Lasagna continued

Drain water off and place walnuts in a food processor, add spices, garlic and onion and mix until chunky and looks similar to ground meat.

Marinara Sauce

Soak dried tomatoes in olive oil (or water) for 30 minutes.

Prepare marinara sauce by placing soaked dried tomatoes with oil in a blender. Add tomatoes into quarters, onion and spice blend until smooth.

Cheese Sauce

Place cashews in a blender, add garlic, seasoning and olive oil then mix, adding water in small amounts until a sauce consistency is achieved. You may need less or more than a cup, depending on the blender used.

Vegetables

Wash spinach and removing the stems and chop bell pepper. You can use yellow, red, or orange bell pepper or combination thereof. You can make this as deluxe as you would like by adding any other vegetables of choice.

Putting it Together

Place a third of the marinara sauce on bottom of a 9x9 pan. Add half of the meatless on top. Using a spoon mix the meatless and marinara. Spread it until it is even.

Layer half of the zoodles over top of the meatless layer, then evenly spread half of the cheese sauce over the zoodles.

Evenly spread vegetables over the cheese sauce. Mix ½ of the remaining marinara with the other half of the meatless and layer over the vegetables.

Top remaining zoodles over the meatless, then spread cheese sauce over the zoodles. Evenly spread the remaining marinara and to with a sprinkling of pumpkin seeds.

Place in a dehydrator at 100° for about 4 hours or until warm.

Collard Herb Rolls

Preparation: *Sprouting:* Makes 4-6
15 Min. 1-4 Days Servings

Ingredients

- 4-6 large collard green leaves or kale leaves
- 2 ½ c. Spicy Nut Cheese (page 112)
- 2 small zucchinis, sliced
- 2 avocadoes, sliced
- 2 tomatoes, sliced
- redish and broccoli sprouts

Directions

Sprout reddish and broccoli sprouts.

Make Spicy Nut Cheese, then wash and prepare the vegetables.

Choose the largest collard green or kale leaves, wash and dry with a paper towel, then cut off stems and set aside.

Spread about ½ cup of Spicy Nut Cheese along each leaf spine, then layer zucchini, avocado, tomatoes and sprouts. Roll up leaves, pate and serve.

Fun Fact:

Collard greens date back to prehistoric times and are one of the oldest members of the cabbage family. The Greeks and Romans grew collards in domestic gardens over 2,000 years ago. Today, collard greens are grown and eaten regularly in many countries across the world, mostly used as a source of food.

Impossible Zucchini Pie

Ingredients

Crust:

- 1 c. golden flax seed, ground in a coffee grinder
- 1 c. buckwheat, soaked
- 1 tbsp. Himalayan crystal salt
- 1-2 c. pure water
- ¼ c. raw coconut flour (optional)

Filling:

- 1 c. Spicy Nut Cheese (page 112)
- 4 tbsp. cold pressed olive oil
- 3 c. zucchini, grated
- 1 large onion, chopped
- ½ red bell pepper, chopped
- 1 c. parsley, chopped
- 1 carrot, shredded
- 2 stocks celery, thinly sliced

Directions

Make the Spicy Nut Cheese and set aside.

Cover buckwheat with pure water and soak for at least 1 hour, (may soak overnight if desired), then drain and rinse the buckwheat. Place buckwheat in a food processor.

Grind flax in a coffee grinder and add into food processor. Mix and add the salt, using only enough water to make dough.

Roll dough out into a circle on a thin cutting board (this makes it easier to move to the dehydrator tray). Using coconut flour to keep it from sticking (ground flax seed may be used in place of coconut flour).

Once you have a nice round fold up the edges, so the crust will hold the filling. Move to dehydrator tray and dry for about an hour.

Grate zucchini and carrots and place in a bowl. Chop onion and parsley add to the zucchini and carrots. Thinly slice bell pepper and celery add spicy nut cheese then add to the bowl and gently mix all vegetates together.

Place zucchini mixture in the prepared crust and dehydrate at 100° for another 3-5 hours.

Impossible Zucchini Pie

Makes 4-6 Servings

Preparation Time:
 15
 Minutes

Drying Time:
 3-5
 Hours

Impossible pie? Not really, it is very possible and not hard to make. Impossible Pie first became widely known in the 1970s when it was printed on the backs of Bisquick boxes

Stuffed Zucchini Blossoms

Makes 4 Servings

Preparation Time:	Soaking Time:	Drying Time:
20 Minutes	8-12 Hours	7-10 Hours

The yellow-orange squash blossoms are considered a delicacy and are traditionally sautéed or deep-fried. This one is battered and dried.

Stuffed Zucchini Blossoms

Ingredients

- 4 zucchini blossoms

Pate

- ¾ c. pumpkin seeds, soaked overnight
- 3 tbsp. fresh parsley, chopped
- 3 tbsp. fresh lemon, juiced
- ¼ c. tomato, chopped
- 1 tbsp. fresh thyme
- 1 ½ tbsp. chives
- Himalayan crystal salt or sea salt to taste
- pepper, to taste

Batter

- ½ c. buckwheat, soaked overnight
- 2 tsp. cold pressed olive oil
- Himalayan crystal salt or sea salt to taste
- pepper to taste
- pure water as needed

Directions

In a bowl cover pumpkin seeds with water and soak overnight. Drain the water off and place in a food processor, mix until evenly combined.

Grind buckwheat in a coffee grinder, then place in a bowl. Cover and soak buckwheat in pure water and for 6-8 hours (the buckwheat will be a little gooey).

Gently wash blossoms and lay open on a dish.

Add lemon juice to food processor with pumpkin seeds, along with parsley, tomato, thyme, chives, salt and pepper then mix until well combined. Place a scoop of mix in each open blossom.

To buckwheat, add the oil, salt, pepper and mix well. Gradually add water until it looks like a thick pancake batter. Spoon batter over top of the stuffed blossoms.

Place in dehydrator for 7-10 hours.

Asparagus Quiche

Ingredients

Cheese

- ½ c. cashew
- 1 ½ tbsp. lemon, juiced
- 1 tbsp. lemon zest
- 1 clove garlic
- 3 tsp. fennel (optional)
- ¼ tsp. Himalayan crystal salt
- ¼ tsp. black pepper
- 4 tbsp. water

Marinated Asparagus

- ¼ c. asparagus
- 2 tsp. lemon zest
- 1 tsp. rosemary
- 1 tsp. thyme
- 1 tbsp. olive oil
- ½ c. lemon or grapefruit juice

Filling

- ½ c. cheese
- 1 tbsp. psyllium husk
- 2 tbsp. lovage leaves
- ¼ c. red bell pepper
- ¼ c. broccoli
- ¼ c. asparagus
- 1 tbsp. fresh or dried dill
- ½ tsp. Himalayan crystal salt
- 1 tsp. turmeric
- ½ c. zucchini, chopped
- ¼ c. onion, chopped

Directions

Make the cheese by placing the ingredients in a blender and combine until smooth. Wrap in cheesecloth and squeeze out excess liquid. Let ferment overnight, with a weight on it.

Trim the ends of the asparagus then place in a pan or baggie and add the lemon zest, rosemary thyme, olive oil and grapefruit juice let marinate overnight.

Put the quiche together by gradating the zucchini, finely chop the broccoli, bell pepper and onion then place in a bowl. Mix in the cheese, phylum husk, lovage, dill, salt, and turmeric.

Press the quiche into a spring form pan. Top with asparagus and dry for about 3 hours or until set up. Remove quiche from the springform and enjoy.

Asparagus Quiche

Makes 4 Servings

Preparation Time:
20
Minutes

Marinating Time:
8-12
Hours

Drying Time:
2-5
Hours

This recipe is a result of a Raw Food Creativity Challenge that was issued in a Facebook group.

Wild Jambalaya

Makes 4-6 Servings

Preparation Time:
45
Minutes

Sprouting Time:
1-3
Days

There are two main types of jambalaya. The Creole method contains tomatoes while the Southwestern and South Central Louisiana Jambalaya is tomato free.

Wild Jambalaya

Ingredients

- 2 c. wild rice, sprouted

Sauce

- 1-2 cloves garlic
- 2 ½ c. tomatoes
- 1 tsp. oregano, dried
- 1 tbsp. fresh parsley or 1 tsp. dried
- 1 tsp. thyme
- ¼ - ½ small hot pepper
- dash paprika
- ½ tsp. pepper
- ½ tsp. Himalayan crystal salt
- ¼ c. sun-dried tomatoes

Vegetables

- 1 medium red bell pepper, finely chopped
- 1 medium onion, finely chopped
- 2 medium tomatoes, finely chopped
- 1 c. zucchini, finely chopped
- ½ c. celery, finely chopped
- 1 c. broccoli florets
- 8-10 mushrooms, sliced (optional)

Directions

Sprout wild rice (page 122) and set aside.

In a blender, mix garlic, tomatoes, oregano, parsley, thyme, hot pepper, paprika, pepper salt and sun-dried tomatoes until well mixed.

Chop bell pepper, onion, tomatoes, zucchini, celery and broccoli mix in a bowl.

Pour blender sauce over vegetables and mix. Stir in the rice and serve right away or let sit for a couple of hours.

Kale Burger

Ingredients

- 2 c. Brazil nuts, soaked
- 1 c. carrots, shredded
- ½ lemon, juiced
- 1 tbsp. garlic powder
- 1 tomatoes
- 1 c. corn
- 1 red bell pepper, chopped
- ¼ c. parsley
- 1 c. kale
- 1 zucchini, chopped
- 1 c. broccoli, chopped
- 1 tbsp. celery seed
- ½ tbsp. poultry seasoning
- ¼ c. dried onion
- ½ c. raw tahini
- 1 tbsp. slippery elm powder
- Himalayan crystal salt to taste

Directions

Soak Brazil nuts in water overnight, drain water, and set aside.

In a food processor, combine Brazil nuts, carrots, tomatoes, corn, red bell pepper, parsley, kale, zucchini, broccoli, lemon juice, tahini, garlic, and spices until mixed thoroughly.

Shape into burgers and dehydrate on nonstick dehydrator sheets for 2-4 hours. Flip and carefully remove the nonstick dehydrator sheet. Continue drying for another 2-4 hours.

Place on some lettuce leaves or in a cabbage leaf and top with avocados and tomatoes.

Kale Burger

Makes 4-6 Servings

Preparation Time:
20
Minutes

Soaking Time:
8-12
Hours

Drying Time:
4-12
Hours

Eating kale with fatty foods like avocado makes it easier for the body to absorb it's nutrients.

Eggplant Kebabs

Makes 4-6 Servings

Preparation Time: Marinating Time: Drying Time:
30   2-12   4-8
Minutes   Hours   Hours

Kebab actually means 'to rosast.' Some say that kebabs are traced to Turkey where soldiers skewered food on their swords to grill on open fires. Others say they are traced to Asian and African Cuisine.

Eggplant Kebabs

Ingredients

- 1 lime, juiced
- 2 tsp. cumin seeds, ground
- 1 tsp. Himalayan crystal salt
- ¼ tsp. cayenne
- ¾ c. nut mayo (page 109)
- 1 eggplant
- 1 yellow bell pepper
- 1 red bell pepper
- ½ medium onion
- 2 medium zucchinis
- 1 clove garlic
- 1 tbsp. ginger
- ½ tsp. raw apple cider vinegar
- ¼ tsp. turmeric
- ½ tsp. coconut liquid aminos (optional)

Directions

Cut eggplant into 1 inch thick rounds, then quartered cut into wedges and set aside.

In a blender, place garlic, ginger, lime, cumin, salt, nut mayo, turmeric, cayenne and blend until well mixed.

Pour marinade over cut eggplant and let sit for 4-8 hours.

Place marinated eggplant onto a dehydrator and dry for about 10-12 hours.

Cut the onion, yellow and red bell peppers into wedges. Slice the zucchini into rounds place the vegetables in a bowl or jar and marinate for 4-8 hours.

Thread eggplant, bell pepper, onion, and zucchini onto skewers. Place in dehydrator for about 7 hours.

Crabby Cakes

Ingredients

- 3 zucchinis, shredded
- 1 green onion, chopped
- ½ tsp. Himalayan crystal salt
- ¼ tsp. pepper
- ½ red, yellow or orange bell pepper, chopped
- 1 clove garlic, finely chopped
- ¼ c. nut mayo (page 109)
- 2 tsp. mustard seed, ground
- 1 lemon, juiced
- 2 celery stalks, thinly sliced
- 1 tsp. kelp

Directions

Make the mayo and set aside.

Shred zucchini and mix with green onion, bell pepper, garlic and place in a bowl. Mix salt, pepper, lemon juice, celery, mustard, kelp, nut mayo and combine mix well using hands.

Take shredded zucchini mixture and shape into a ½ inch thick patties. Place patties on the dehydrator with nonstick sheet. Dry at 100° for about 2 hours.

Flip and remove nonstick sheet, then continue drying until desired dryness is achieved.

Fun Fact:

The witches in Macbeth made eye of newt famous. However, did you know that **mustard seed** used to be known as eye of newt.

Crabby Cakes

Makes 4-6 Servings

Preparation Time:
40
Minutes

Drying Time:
1 - 3
Hours

The first crab cake recipe by Crosby Gaige called Baltimore crab cake published in the 1930s. This recipe replaces the crab with zucchini.

Zucchini Sticks

Makes 4-6 Servings

Preparation Time:
30
Minutes

Soaking Time:
6 - 8
Hours

Drying Time:
3 - 6
Hours

Fried zucchini is typically cut to the size and shape of fries, then battered and fried. This is my version of the traditional fried zucchini sticks.

Zucchini Sticks

Ingredients

Batter

- 1 c. buckwheat, ground in a coffee grinder
- 1 tbsp. cold pressed olive oil
- 2 tsp. Himalayan crystal salt
- ½ tsp. turmeric
- 1 lemon, juiced
- 1 orange, juiced
- 1 c. pure water
- paprika (optional)

Sticks

- 3 zucchinis, cut into strips

Directions

Grind buckwheat in a coffee grinder, then place in a bowl. Soak buckwheat in pure water for 60 minutes, (the buckwheat will be a little gooey).

Place the buckwheat in a blender add lemon and orange juices, turmeric and salt then blend until smooth.

Place zucchini sticks on dehydrator tray with a nonstick sheet.

Spoon batter over the of each zucchini stick. Sprinkle with paprika, if desired. Dry in dehydrator at 100° F. for 1-3 hours.

Take sticks from the dehydrator and flip over. Pour more batter over top, sprinkle with paprika, and continue to dry for another 1-3 hours.

Note: Serve zucchini sticks with fry sauce (page 111).

Zucchini Pizza

Ingredients

Crust:

- 1 c. golden flax seed, ground in a coffee grinder
- 1 c. buckwheat, soaked
- 1 tbsp. Himalayan crystal salt
- 1-2 c. pure water
- ¼ c. raw coconut flour (optional)

Sauce:

- 3 tomatoes, chopped
- 1 tbsp. pizza seasoning
- 1 tbsp. olive oil

Topping:

- 1 zucchini, thinly sliced
- 1 red or yellow bell pepper, sliced
- ½ c. sun dried olives
- ½ c. artichokes hearts (optional)
- 1 c. nut mayo (page 109)

Directions

Make the nut mayo and set aside.

Place tomatoes, pizza seasoning and olive oil in a blender and mix into sauce.

Soak buckwheat for at least 1 hour, (can soak overnight if desired), drain the water and rinse the buckwheat. Place the buckwheat in a food processor.

Grind flax seeds in a coffee grinder and add to the food processor. Mix add salt and just enough water to make a pizza dough.

Roll the dough out into a circle, using the coconut flour to keep from sticking. This step could be done with ground flax seed as well.

Wash and slice the zucchini and bell peppers and chop the artichoke hearts.

Place sauce on the dough. Layer artichoke hearts, zucchini, bell peppers and olives. Top with dollops of mayo, (this becomes cheese).

Dry at 100° in a dehydrator for an hour or two.

Note: The crust works best if the kitchen is warm.

Desserts

Spice Cake with Green Carob Pudding

Chocolate Zucchini Cake

Makes 6-8 Servings

Preparation Time:
40
Minutes

Soaking Time:
4-12
Hours

Drying Time:
4-12
Hours

If you have extra zucchinis or even if you do not this cake is a good way to sneak zucchini into the diet of people who would not otherwise eat it.

Chocolate Zucchini Cake

Ingredients

- 2 ½ c. pecans, soaked in water overnight
- 1 c. dates, soaked 20 minutes
- ½ c. prunes, soaked 20 minutes
- 1 c. zucchini, finely grated
- 1 tsp. Himalayan crystal salt or sea salt
- 2 tsp. cinnamon
- 1 tbsp. vanilla or vanilla bean
- 1 c. raw carob
- carob frosting (page 100)

Directions

Cover pecans with water and soak overnight, then drain and set aside.

Place nuts in a food processor and mix until they are broken into small pieces. Add dates, prunes, zucchini, vanilla, spices and mix until well combined.

Grate zucchini, then add to nuts mixture and mix until evenly distributed.

Shape into 2 or 3 rounds about ½ inch high and place on a dehydrator tray with non-stick sheets.

Dehydrate for 4 hours. Flip and remove the non-stick dehydrator sheet and continue drying at 100° F for about another 4 hours or until desired dryness is achieved.

Remove and decorate with Carob Frosting.

Fun Fact:

The **carob** tree, also known as honey locust, and "St. John's Bread" is an evergreen, native to the Mediterranean and can live to be 100 years old.

Pistachio Pudding

Ingredients

- ¾ c. raw pistachio nuts, shelled and soaked overnight
- 3 c. small zucchinis, chopped
- 2 medium avocados, peeled
- 2 medium bananas, peeled
- ½ - ¾ c. pitted dates, soaked
- 1 tbsp. pure vanilla extract (optional not a raw product)

Directions

Cover with water and soak shelled pistachio overnight, drain water and set aside.

Soak dates for at least 30 minutes. May need longer soaking time, if they are very hard and drain. Retain water for later uses.

Place dates in a food processor until it forms a paste. Use date water as needed to achieve a creamy texture.

To the food processor add ¼ cup of the pistachios, and all the pitted avocado, bananas, zucchini and blend until smooth.

Add remaining pistachios and pulse a few times. This may be chunky with nuts. If you want it to be smoother add all the pistachios before mixing with the avocado mix.

Fun Fact:

Pistachios are one the oldest flowering nut trees native to the Middle East. Archeological evidence shows humans have eaten pistachios since 7,000 B.C.

The Queen of Sheba, according to legend, loved pistachios so much she declared them for royalty only. She even forbade the growing of them by commoners.

Pistachio Pudding

Makes 4-6 Servings

Preparation Time:
15
Minutes

Legends says that King Nebuchadnezzar planted pistachio trees were grown in the hanging gardens of Babylon, one of the Seven Wonders of the World.

Zucchini Carrot Cake

Makes 6-8 Servings

Preparation Time:
40
Minutes

Soaking Time:
4-12
Hours

Drying Time:
4-12
Hours

Carrot cake is good, but when zucchini is added it is even better.

Zucchini Carrot Cake

Ingredients

- 2 ½ c. walnuts, soaked overnight
- ¼ c. shredded coconut, unsweetened
- ½ c. prunes
- 1 c. dates, pitted
- ½ c. raisins
- 2 c. zucchini, grated
- 2 c. carrot, grated
- ½ tsp. Himalayan crystal salt or sea salt
- ¼ tsp. ground nutmeg
- ¼ tsp. ground ginger
- 1 tsp. cinnamon
- 1 ½ tsp. vanilla or vanilla bean
- cream frosting
- carrot curls for decoration.

Directions

Cover walnuts with water and soak overnight, then drain.

Place walnuts in a food processor, along with zucchini, vanilla, nutmeg, ginger, cinnamon, salt and mix until combined.

Add prunes, dates and coconut to the walnuts and mix until combined.

Place grated zucchini and half of the grated carrots in with the nuts and mix until evenly distributed. Stir in the remaining carrots and the raisins.

Shape into 2 or 3 rounds about ½ inch high, on a dehydrator tray on top a non-stick dehydrator sheets. Dehydrate for 4 hours. Flip and remove the non-stick dehydrator sheet and continue drying at 100° F for about another 4 hours or until desired moisture is achieved.

Remove and decorate with Cream Frosting and carrot curls.

Spice Cake with Green Carob Pudding

Ingredients

- date cream frosting (page 98)

Spice Cake

- 1 c. zucchini, shredded
- 1 c. kohlrabi, shredded
- 1 c. apple, chopped
- 4 tsp. shallot, chopped
- 1 c. dates
- 2 tsp. vanilla
- 1 c. walnuts, soaked
- 1 tbsp. raw almond butter
- 3 tbsp. flax seed or psyllium husk powder
- 1 tsp. nutmeg, ground
- ½ tsp. Himalayan crystal salt
- 1 tsp. cinnamon, ground
- 1 ½ tsp. ginger, ground
- 1 tsp. cloves, ground

Green Carob Pudding

- 1 c. spinach, chopped
- 1 avocado, pitted
- ¼ c. raw carob
- ½ c. dates
- 1 c. water

Directions

Cover walnuts nuts with water and soak overnight, then drain and place in a food processor. Pit the dates and place in a food processor with walnuts along with the zucchini, kohlrabi, apple, shallot, mushroom, vanilla, almond butter, psyllium husk, salt, nutmeg, cinnamon, ginger, cloves and mix well.

Separate the cake into thirds and make each into equal sized rounds on nonstick dehydrator sheets. Dry for about 4 hours. Flip the cakes over and remove the nonstick dehydrator sheet and continue drying for another 6 to 8 hours, until desired texture and dryness is achieved.

Make the pudding by pitting and soaking dates in water for 30 minutes, then drain and retain water. In a blender, mix spinach, avocado meat, soaked dates and carob. Use the date soaking water as needed to achieve a smooth texture.

Decorate with the date cream frosting and cover the cake.

Spice Cake with Green Carob Pudding

Makes 6-8 Servings

Preparation Time:
30
Minutes

Drying:
8-12
Hours

The raw carob I used is light tan in color and so the green color came through. If your carob is brown you will have a chocolate looking pudding.

95

Sweet Kale Cheesecake

Makes 6-8 Servings

Preparation Time:
35
Minutes

Chillng:
3-5
Hours

This dessert is a good way to hide vegetables in something sweet to eat. This kale cheesecake is topped off with candied kale.

Sweet Kale Cheesecake

Ingredients

Cheesecake

- ½ c. cashews
- ½ c. macadamia nuts
- 1 c. kale, chopped
- ½ c. zucchini, chopped
- ½ c. coconut oil
- ½ c. raw coconut nectar
- ¼ tsp. Himalayan crystal salt
- 2 tbsp. lemon juice
- ¼ c. water

Crust

- 1 c. pecans
- ½ c. dates

Directions

Place pecans, which have been soaked and dried (see appendix), in a food processor, add pitted dates and blend until well mixed. Press crust into a spring form pan.

In a food processor or high-power blender place cashews, macadamia nuts, zucchini, kale, coconut oil, coconut nectar, lemon juice, salt and blend until smooth. Add water, as needed, to achieve a thick smooth texture.

Pour mixture onto crust and freeze for at least 5 hours. Decorate with candied kale (page 98). Keep refrigerated.

Note

This can be made with either all cashews or macadamia nuts.

Candied Kale

Preparation: 20 Min.   *drying:* 1-2 Hrs.   *Makes 6-8 Servings*

Ingredients

- 1 bunch kale
- 1 tbsp. cold pressed olive oil
- 3 tbsp. coconut nectar
- 1 tsp. Himalayan crystal salt

Directions

Using a knife or kitchen shears carefully remove kale leaves from their thick stems and tear into large pieces. Wash and thoroughly dry kale pieces.

In a bowl, mix the coconut nectar, olive oil and salt. Massage the oil mixture into the kale.

Place the kale on a dehydrator tray in a single layer and dry for about an hour. Chips should be crispy when done.

Date Cream Frosting

Preparation: 20 Min.   *Makes 6-8 Servings*

Ingredients

- 1 c. cashews
- ½ c. raw coconut oil
- ½ c. dates
- ¼ tsp. vanilla
- ¼ - ¾ c. water
- 1 tsp. cinnamon, ground (optional)

Directions

Cover pitted dates with ¾ cup water for 30 minutes.

Place cashews, coconut oil, dates, cinnamon and vanilla in a blender or food processor. Use date water, as needed, to reach a smooth frosting.

Zucchini Cookies

Preparation: 20 Min. Soaking: 4-12 Hr. Drying: 7-12 Hrs. Makes 4-6 Servings

Ingredients

- 1 c. walnuts, soaked overnight
- ¾ c. dates, pitted
- 1 c. zucchini, shredded
- 1 tsp. cinnamon
- ¼ c. oat flour or coconut flour
- 1 tsp. pure vanilla
- pinch of Himalayan crystal salt
- ½ c. raisins

Directions

Cover buckwheat and walnuts in separate bowls with water, soak overnight then drain and place in food processor, add the zucchini, dates, cinnamon, vanilla, salt and nutmeg in the food processor and blend until smooth adding small amounts of fresh water, as needed. Place into a bowl.

Grind oat groats in a coffee grinder to make oat flour. Add oat flour and raisins to the zucchini mixture, mix until well combined.

Place mixture on your dehydrator tray with non-stick dehydrator sheets, spread into ¼-inch thick rounds.

Dry at 105° F for about 3 hours. Flip and remove the non-stick dehydrator sheets and continue to dry for about 2-4 more hours or until they are dry and cookie consistency.

Variation

Chocolate Chunk Zucchini Cookies

Chop up frozen cacao fudge into chunks and mix in the above cookie dough.

Fudge recipe

- ½ c. unrefined raw coconut oil • ½ c raw liquid sweetener • ¾ c. raw cacao powder • 2 tsp. pure vanilla • pinch cayenne • pinch salt

Mix all ingredients and then place in freezer.

Carob Frosting

Preparation: *Makes 4-6*
10 Min. *Servings*

Ingredients

- 1 c. raw carob or raw cacao powder
- ½ c. raw liquid sweetener (coconut nectar, agave etc.)
- 1 tbsp. vanilla (optional--not a raw product) or vanilla bean
- ¾ - 1 c. water

Directions

Place carob powder, and sweetener in a bowl, add vanilla and slowly add water, mixing constantly until the desired thickness is achieved. You may add more carob if desired.

Note: If you are using cacao nibs then grind them in a coffee grinder first.

Cream Frosting

Preparation: *Makes 4-6*
10 Min. *Servings*

Ingredients

- 1 c. macadamia nuts
- ½ c. raw coconut oil
- ½ c. raw liquid sweetener (coconut nectar, agave etc.)
- ¾ - 1 c. water

Directions

Place macadamia nuts, coconut oil and sweetener to the food processor and mix until evenly combined. Add water, until desired thickness and smoothness is achieved.

Miscellaneous

Zucchini Chips

Zucchini Carrot Bread Sticks

Makes 4-6 Servings

Preparation Time:
20
Minutes

Drying Time:
3-8
Hours

Zucchini bread is a well-known summer food. This recipe includes carrots and is more savory than traditionally sweet zucchini bread

Zucchini Carrot Bread Sticks

Ingredients

- 1 tbsp. chia or flaxseed, ground
- ¾ c. cashews
- 2 tbsp. sesame seeds, ground
- 1 c. carrots, grated
- 2 c. zucchini, grated
- ¼ c. onion, chopped finely
- 1 cloves, garlic
- ¼ - ½ c. coconut flour
- 2 tbsp. nutritional yeast (optional)

Directions

Soak cashew for 20 minutes for a creamery dough.

Combine ground chia or flax with 2 tablespoon water and set aside for 5 minutes.

In a blender, combine the soaked flax seeds, cashews, sesame seeds, onion, garlic, and nutritional yeast until smooth. Add a dash of water, if needed, to make the mixture smoother.

Shred zucchini and carrots and place in a large bowl and combine with cashew mixture. Add coconut flour to the mix until well combined.

Spread mixture evenly on dehydrator tray, and dry for 4 to 6 hours. Flip and remove the non-stick sheet half way through drying.

When dried to desired texture (dry but not hard), cut into slices and serve.

Note

This bread can be used as a pizza crust if dried longer and add toppings.

Zucchini Crackers

Preparation: 40 Min. *Soaking:* 6-8 Hrs. *Drying:* 4-8 Hrs. *Makes 4-6 Servings*

Ingredients

- 1 c. raw sunflower seed, soaked
- 1 c. raw pumpkin seeds, soaked
- 2 carrots, shredded
- 1 red bell pepper, finely chopped
- 1 onion, finely chopped
- 3 celery stocks, chopped
- 1 medium zucchini, finely shredded
- 1-2 cloves garlic
- 1 tomato
- 1 tsp. caraway seeds
- 1 tsp. coriander seed
- 1 tsp. Himalayan crystal salt or sea salt

Directions

Cover sunflower and pumpkin seeds with water and soak at 6-10 hours, then drain the water off and place in a food processor.

Add carrots and spices to the seed mixture and combine until finely mixed.

Add bell pepper, onion, celery, zucchini, garlic and tomato to the food processor and mix.

Spread mixture on a non-stick dehydrator sheet until about ¼ inch thick. Dry at 100° F for about 4 hours. Flip and remove the non-stick dehydrator sheet.

Continue drying until desired crispness is obtained.

Ricotta Cheese Sauce

Preparation: 15 Min. Makes 4-6 Servings

Ingredients

- 1 c. macadamia nuts
- 2 cloves garlic
- 1 ½ tsp. Himalayan crystal salt or sea salt
- 2 tsp. Italian seasoning
- ½ c. zucchini
- ½ c. water or more, as needed

Directions

In a blender, puree the macadamia nuts, garlic, zucchini, and spice until fluffy, while using as little water as possible to appear like cheese sauce.

Zucchini Chips

Preparation: 15 Min. Drying: 3-6 Hrs. Makes 4-6 Servings

Ingredients

- 4 small zucchinis, thinly sliced into rounds
- ½ c. cold pressed olive oil
- 1 tbsp. Himalayan crystal salt or sea salt
- 2 tsp. turmeric
- 1 tsp. paprika (optional)

Directions

Wash and cut the zucchini into rounds and set aside. In a small bowl, mix oil, salt, turmeric and paprika.

Place rounds on dehydrator sheets and brush oil mixture on top. Turn them over and bush on the other side.

Dehydrate at 100° F 3-6 hours or until desired crispness is obtained.

Zucchini Bagles

Ingredients

- 1 c. buckwheat, ground
- ½ c. raw coconut four
- ½ c. flaxseeds, ground
- 1 c. walnuts, ground
- 2 tbsp. chia seeds
- ¾ c. zucchini, peeled
- 1 clove garlic
- 2 tbsp. onion
- 2 tbsp. coconut nectar
- 1 lemon, juiced
- 1 c. water
- ¼ c. cashews
- 2 tbsp. nutritional yeast (optional)
- herbed vegan cream cheese (page 113, optional topping)

Directions

Place walnuts in a food processor and mix until a flour is formed. Grind flaxseeds and buckwheat in a coffee grinder and add to the food processor, along with chia seeds and set aside.

In a blender, place zucchini, garlic, onion, coconut nectar, lemon juice, water, cashews, and nutritional yeast and mix until creamy.

Pour blender ingredients into the food processor with the dry ingredients and mix until it looks like a soft dough.

Spread on counter with more coconut flour and knead until dough is not sticky. Let the dough rest for 10-20 minutes.

Use about ¼ cup to form each bagel into a ball. Flatten the balls and make a hole in the middle with your finger for bagel shape, (or a donut pan).

Place on a dehydrator and dry about 2 hours. Cut each bagel in half and continue drying for another 2 or so hours. It is ready when the desired texture is achieved.

Zucchini Bagels

Makes 6-8 Servings

Preparation Time:
30
Minutes

Drying:
8-12
Hours

I was so disappointed when I thought I would never have a bagel again. This recipe is a good replacement.

Almond Mayo

Makes 4-6 Servings

Preparation Time:
30
Minutes

Drying Time:
2-6
Hours

Mayonnaise or Mayo is traditionally made with eggs and oil. This mayo is a vegan replacement using nuts in place of eggs.

Almond Mayo

Preparation: 10 Min.   *Soaking: 8-12 Hrs.*   *Makes 6-8 Servings*

Ingredients

- 2 c. almonds, soaked overnight
- 3 tbsp. onion powder
- ½ c. cold pressed olive oil
- ¾ c. water
- 1-2 tbsp. Himalayan crystal salt
- ½ lemon, juiced

Directions

Cover almonds with water, soak overnight and drain. While still wet peel the brown shell off each almond. You will have whitish almonds.

Place peeled almonds into a blender and add olive oil, onion powder, salt, and lemon juice.

Slowly blend adding enough water until a creamy, mayo consistency is achieved.

Variations

For cashew mayo substitute cashew nuts for almonds and omit orange juice. Cashews can become rubbery, so I usually do not soak them very long if at all.

This recipe can be used with almost any nut or seed you can think of. For example, hazelnut, pumpkin seeds, walnuts etc.

Fun Fact:

Cashews have about 553 calories for 100 grams. However, they are also high in heart-friendly monounsaturated fatty acid and are an abundant source of minerals; including selenium and copper.

Almond Mylk

Preparation: *Soaking:*   *Makes 6-8*
5 Min.   *8-12 Hrs.*   *Servings*

Ingredients

- 1 C. almonds, soaked overnight
- 2 C. pure water

Directions

Cover almond with water and soak overnight, drain off the water and place into a blender with 2 cups of pure fresh water. Blend for a minute or two.

Using a mylk bag, (clean nylon sock, or cheesecloth) over a big bowl, pour contents of the blender into the bag.

Then squeeze out liquid for mylk and sweeten mylk if desired.

Note: if you want to use the almond pulp in another recipe such as almond mayo, cookies, crackers or bread just peel off the brown skin.

Variation

Nut mylk may be made with any nut or seed that you can imagine such as Brazil nuts, pumpkin seeds, and hazelnut to name a few.

Guacamole

Preparation: *Makes 4-6*
15 Min.   *Servings*

Ingredients

- ¼ c. mayo (page 109)
- 1-2 large avocados, pitted
- Himalayan crystal salt or sea salt to taste

Directions

Make mayo and set aside.

remove avocado from the shell and place on a plate, add mayo and salt and mix with a fork.

Almond Sour Cream

Preparation: 15 Min. Makes 4-6 Servings

Ingredients

- 1 c. almonds, soaked
- 1 tsp. lemon juice
- 1 tbsp. raw apple cider vinegar
- ½ c. pure water as needed
- Himalayan crystal salt or natural sea salt to taste

Directions

Cover almonds with water and soak overnight and drain. While skins are still wet, peel off the skin to create a white sour cream. If the skin remains, you will have a brown flaked sour cream.

In a blender combine the peeled almonds, lemon juice, raw apple cider vinegar, and salt. Purée until creamy, adding only enough water, as needed.

Taste and adjust seasoning adding more lemon or vinegar if not sour enough.

Fry Sauce

Preparation: 15 Min. Makes 4-6 Servings

Ingredients

- 1 medium zucchini, chopped
- 1 tomato, chopped
- ¼ tsp. mustard seed powder
- 1 tsp. cold pressed olive oil
- 2 tsp. lemon, juiced
- 1 tsp. onion powder
- Himalayan crystal salt to taste
- pepper, to taste

Directions

In a blender, mix zucchini, tomato, lemon juice, vinegar, cashews and spices until creamy. Serve with fries or use any other time as you would fry sauce.

Spicy Nut Cheese

Preparation: 15 Min. Soaking: 8-12 Hrs. Makes 6-8 Servings

Ingredients

- 2 c. almonds, soaked overnight
- ½ c. lemon juice
- ½ tsp. Himalayan crystal salt or sea salt
- 1 tsp. fresh dill
- ½ c. green onion, chopped
- 1 red bell pepper, diced
- 1 chili pepper
- ½ c. dried tomatoes

Directions

Cover almonds with water and soak overnight, then drain.

In a small bowl, cover dried tomatoes in water let soak for 30 min. Fresh tomatoes may also be used. Then drain and save tomato water for later use if needed (**don't** use the almond water).

In a food processor, place almonds, lemon juice, salt, dill, green onion, red bell pepper, and chili pepper and combine until well mixed. Add dried tomatoes and blend until incorporated. Chill and serve.

Note

Serving Suggestion

Serve on a flax cracker or other raw crackers or as dip with vegetables.

Herbed Vegan Cream Cheese

Preparation: 20 Min.   Soaking: 2-8 hrs.   Makes 2-4 Servings

Ingredients

- ½ c. cashews
- ½ c. pumpkin seeds, soaked overnight
- 2 lemons, juiced
- ½ tsp. Himalayan crystal salt
- ¼ tsp. nutritional yeast (optional)
- ½ tsp. chives
- ½ tsp. dried oregano
- ½ tsp. dried parsley
- ½ tsp. dried basil
- ¼ tsp. dried dill

Directions

Cover pumpkin seeds with water and soak overnight, then drain and pace in a food processor.

Soak the cashews in water for 10 minutes, drain and add to pumpkin seeds.

Add lemon juice to the food processor, along with salt, nutritional yeast, chives, oregano, parsley, basil and dill then process until smooth. Add water, a tablespoon at a time, to thin the mixture, if needed.

Place in a dish cover and chill for about an hour or until ready to serve. May store in a sealed container for 4-7 days.

Note

This may also be made with all cashews if desired.

Sassy Hot Sauce

Preparation: 30 Min. *Makes 4-6 Servings*

Ingredients

- 2 medium zucchinis, chopped
- ¼ c. onion, chopped
- 1 clove garlic
- 1 lemon, juiced
- 1 tsp. Himalayan crystal salt or sea salt
- ¼ tsp. onion powder
- ¼ tsp chili pepper, dried
- ¼ tsp cumin seeds, ground
- ¼ tsp coriander powder
- ¼ tsp cayenne
- ¼ tsp oregano, dried
- ¼ tsp. basil, dried
- ¼ tsp. red chili pepper, dried
- ¼ tsp. celery seed, dried
- ¼ tsp. rosemary, dried
- ¼ tsp. thyme, dried

Directions

Place zucchini, onion, garlic oil and lemon juice in a blender, add salt, onion, chili, cumin, coriander, cayenne, oregano, basil, chili pepper, celery seed, rosemary and thyme and blend until creamy. Add water only if needed to achieve desired thickness.

Note

Fresh herbs may be used in place of dried.

Variation

May add avocado or tomato or both to this sauce.

Tahini

Ingredients

- ¾ c. sesame seeds
- 2 tbsp. cold pressed olive oil
- 1 tsp. Himalayan crystal salt
- 1 lemon, juiced
- ¼ c. water

Directions

Grind sesame seeds in a coffee grinder to make sesame Grind sesame seeds in a coffee grinder to make sesame flour and place in a bowl.

Add salt and lemon juice to flour and mix. Gradually add oil until desired consistency is achieved.

Stores in the fridge up to one month.

Fun Fact:

Tahini is the result of ground sesames seeds blended into a paste or butter.

Sesame is grown primarily for its oil-rich seeds; which come in a variety of colors, from cream to black. Heating damages the healthy poly-unsaturated fats.

It has been said there was sesame seeds found in the tomb of Tutankhamen "King Tut" of Egypt.

Also according to Assyrian legend, when the gods met to create the world, they drank wine made from sesame seeds.

Irish Moss Gel

Ingredients

- 1 c. Irish moss
- 2-3 c. pure water

Directions

Rinse Irish moss. Soak in water for 30 minutes. Drain and rinse again then soak overnight in a glass jar, then drain.

Place Irish moss in a blender with just enough fresh water to cover. Blend until smooth, it may take a few minutes.

Pour into a clean jar with a lid. Store in refrigerator up to 3 weeks.

Fun Fact:

Irish Moss is a tough and stringy seaweed growing that grows on rocks in tidal pools along the northern Atlantic.

It is harvested to make carrageenan, (from the Irish word carraigín meaning "little rock") a thickening agent for jellies, puddings, and soups, and is a traditional herbal remedy in Ireland.

Irish Moss is so nutrient dense that it was used as "poverty food" during the famous Irish Potato Famine of 1846 – 1848. It is thought that this contributed to its fall from favor after the famine.

The human body is made up of 102 minerals and Irish Moss contains a whopping 92 of them. It also provides a wealth of other important nutrients including; protein, beta-carotene, B vitamins, pectin, and vitamin C.

Appendix

Definitions

When you start out on a raw food diet, you may hear a lot of confusing terms. I have compiled a list of some common terms to help you.

Enzyme = is produced by a living organism and functions as a biochemical catalyst. It's major job is to help regulate chemical reactions throughout our lifespan.

An **enzyme inhibitor** is a molecule that binds to enzymes and decreases their activity. They are nature's way of preserving and making nuts, seeds, and grains last for long period of time. (This is why you don't drink the soaking water as is has the enzyme inhibitors from the nut/seeds.)

Raw Food = is food that is raw, not cooked

Some products that are not raw because of the temperature in which they were processed. Some of are: balsamic vinegar, bulgur wheat, couscous, pasteurized juice etc.

Living Food = is food that is freshly picked directly from the plant and is eaten immediately or prepared in a way (such as soaking nuts or sprouting) to activate enzymes.

Sprouts and food eaten right off the vine or tree are examples of living foods.

Whole Foods Plant-Based (WFPB) = is a way of eating that emphasizes whole, minimally processed foods. The focus is on plants that include vegetables, fruits, whole grains, legumes, seeds and nuts.

In the most general terms this would include a vegan and raw food diet.

Whole Foods Plant-Based, No Oil (WFPBNO) = is a version of whole food plant-based diet but excludes all oil.

Transition Food = Food that is used to transition from traditional standard diet to a raw food diet.

Some transition foods include: Maple syrup (grade B or C), Molasses (it has been heated). Some people use bottled ketchup, tofu, veganinase, and sugar; these products are not raw. When going to potlucks, I recommend that you don't use them.

Superfoods = Food that is nutrient rich and beneficial for health.

Superfoods examples include: walnuts, Brussels sprouts, acai berries, cacao, avocadoes etc.

Raw Liquid Sweetener = A raw sweetener that includes, but may not be limited to, coconut nectar, agave nectar, raw honey (not vegan) etc.

When I started it helped me to think about the way I made food in the following conversions:

Food Preparation = cook

Cook = prepare

Fry = warm, no greater than 110 degrees

Boil = soak

Bake = dehydrate

When most raw food recipes call for nuts, they mean soaked nuts, unless otherwise stated; hard nuts like almonds 12-24 hours, soft nuts 4-6 hours. After nuts have been soaked, the enzymes are active, and the nuts will spoil if not used in a day or two. Keep them refrigerated after soaking.

One thing I like to do with my nuts is to soak and then dehydrate them, so they are ready to use and have a longer shelf life.

Remember that 70% of what you eat or drink should be deep green, (kale, lettuce, wheat grass, etc.) the darker the green, the better. Sprouts and clean water are very important as well.

Salt

Salt is essential for life -- you cannot live without it. There are enormous differences between the standard, refined table salt and natural salt.

Table salt is manufactured sat that is stripped of its natural minerals. Salt is not a dangerous food, however the in the process of refining table salt the balance of sodium in comparison to other minerals is lost. Then the to keep salt from clumping anti-caking agents are added. One of the most common parts of anti-caking contain aluminum.

You don't have to eliminate salt entirely just the refined table salt. The alternative is unrefined sea salt (natural sea salt). These salts retain minerals other than just sodium that are good for the body.

In short, the differences in refined and unrefined salt can have a major impact on health. The body recognizes common table salt as poison and has nothing in common with natural salt. If you want your body to function properly, you need complete salt with all-natural elements.

My preferred salt is Himalayan Crystal Salt (it is pink in color).

The Fresenius Institute in Europe analyzed the Himalayan Crystal Salt and found that it has an amazing array of important trace minerals and elements including; potassium, calcium and magnesium. These minerals help your body achieve balance by restoring fluids and replenishing your supply of electrolytes when sweating heavily.

Celtic salt is another popular unrefined and is grayish in color.

Real salt (Redmond) is unrefined and the only pink salt and mined in America.

Sea salt is a better option, but there is a need to be careful as 89% of all sea salt producers now refine their salt. Therefore, sea salt is not quite as healthy as it used to be. (Remember, that our oceans are being used as dumping grounds for harmful toxic poisons).

Sprouting

Sprouting happens when a seed germinates and begins to grow. Energy is released, and natural chemical changes occur, so they become easier for the human body to assimilate. They are also a convenient way to have fresh vegetables in any season and grown in your home.

There are many methods of sprouting (jar, paper-towel, and tray). Start all sprouting by soaking seeds overnight in water, drain the water and place the seeds in your jar or tray. Water seeds 2 times a day, make sure the water completely drains or they will rot and not grow. The sprouts are ready when they start growing tails (1 to 6 days). Sprouts keep up to a week in a refrigerator.

Note: Some beans' sprouts, such as pinto beans, are very bitter when eaten raw. If you must have your pinto beans, sprout them, then lightly steam them to remove bitterness.

Some plants, such as those belonging to the nightshade family, (tomato, potato, peppers, eggplant etc.), should not have their sprouts eaten. The fruit of the nightshade is safe to eat, but the green sprouts are poisonous. These plants have a substance called solanine, which protects them from being eating by insects before they are ripe. This is why nightshade sprouts are not eaten.

Sprouting Rice

Wild rice is not really rice it is the seed of an aquatic grass. There are four species of wild rice. One is native to Asia it is harvested at a vegetable. The other three are found in the Great Lakes region and harvested as a grain.

Black wild rice will sprout by soaking it in water and changing the water. This differs from other sprouts because rice grows in water.

The process is very simple: Soak 1-2 cups of rice in water overnight, then drain and rinse and add fresh water. Rinse the rice every day keeping it covered in water 2-4 days (the length of sprouting time may vary based on climactic factors). The rice is ready to eat when it is soft and easy to chew, some wild black rice will split down the middle.

Brown rice can be sprouted but does not taste very good in my opinion. White rice will not sprout as the germ has been removed.

Drying Nuts/Seeds

After soaking the nuts and seeds to release the enzyme inhibitors, I like to dehydrate the ones I am not using in a recipe right away.

Once the nuts are soaked, they will spoil. By drying them, they keep for a longer time and they are ready for use when needed. Dehydrate them at 100° F for about 18 hours.

Olive Oil

"Expeller Pressed" is a continuous feed method where oil is squeezed from the raw material in one step under high pressure. All cold pressed oil is expeller pressed, but not all expeller pressed oil is cold pressed. If the bottle says expeller pressed, it may or may not have been processed under high heat. The only way to know for sure is to call the manufacturer or the label clearly states "cold pressed".

Olive Oil Labeling

What does the labeling on olive oil mean?

Extra-virgin olive oil (EVOO) comes from the first pressing of olives, contains no more than 0.8% acidity, and is judged to have a superior taste. There can be no refined oil in extra-virgin olive oil.

Virgin olive oil has an acidity less than 2% and is judged to have a good taste. There can be no refined oil in virgin olive oil.

Olive oil is a blend of virgin oil and refined virgin oil, containing at most 1% acidity. It commonly lacks a strong flavor.

Olive-pomace oil is a blend of refined pomace olive oil and, possibly, some virgin oil. It is fit for consumption, but it may not be called olive oil. Olive-pomace oil is rarely found in a grocery store as it is often used for certain kinds of cooking in restaurants.

Lampante oil is olive oil which is not used for consumption. Lampante comes from olive oil's ancient use as fuel in oil-burning lamps. Lampante oil is mostly used in the industrial market.

Equipment

The equipment used in this book and common in a raw foods kitchen include:

Mylk Bag: is usually a fine mesh nylon bag with a drawstring. Used to strain out nut pulp from the liquid nut mylk.

Sprouting equipment: I like sprouting trays. You can use the jar method or whatever method you enjoy and with which you have the most success. Check online to learn how to sprout if you don't know how. Then experiment and find the way that works best for you.

Spiralizer: is for making vegetable noodles (zoodles). If you don't have one you can just shred the vegetables by hand or with a potato peeler.

Dehydrator: the type does not really matter much, as long as it has a temperature control on it. I like the square ones where you can remove the trays and place pie pans in them.

Food Processor: This will become your new best friend. Get one that you like and that has enough power to do the job.

Good Blender: Any blender, as long as it is powerful, will work. Even not so powerful ones will work, but the food may not be as creamy or fluffy and may be grittier.

Knives and cutting board, bowls and pans: these are normal things to have in your kitchen and you will want to have a good set to use.

Remember that you don't need all of it at once.

Index

A

A Brief History 6
Almond Delight 35
Almond Delight (photo) 34
Almond Mayo 109
Almond Mayo (photo) 108
Almond Milk 110
Almond Mylk 110
Almond Sour Cream 111
Apple Zucchini Salad 27
Asparagus Quiche 74
Asparagus Quiche
    (photo) 49, 75

B

Bagles 106
Benefits of Zucchini 12
Buttered Zucchini 48
Buttered Zucchini (photo) 15
Butter Sauce 48

C

Cabbage Roll 52
Candied Kale 98
Cardamom Rice 63
Carob 89
Carob Frosting 100
Cashews 109
Cheese Sauce 67
Chocolate Chunk Zucchini
    Cookies 99
Chocolate Zucchini Cake 89
Chocolate Zucchini
    Cake (photo) 88
Collard Herb Rolls 69
Crabby Cakes 82
Crabby Cakes (photo) 83
Cravin' Mac & Cheese 54
Cravin' Mac & Cheese
    (photo) 55
Cream Frosting 100

D

Date Cream Frosting 98
Definitions 118
Dragon Dipping Sauce 61
Dragon Dressing 61
Dragon Eggs 61
Dragon Eggs (photo) 60
Drying Nuts/Seeds 122

E

Eggplant Kebabs 81
Eggplant Kebabs (photo) 80
Equipment 124

F

Flora's Albanian Salad 39
Flora's Albanian
    Salad (photo) 38
Fresh Garden Soup 23
Fry Sauce 111
Fudge 99

G

Gazpacho 22
Green Dressing 45
Green Zoodles 40
Green Zoodles (photo) 41
Guacamole 110

H

Herbed Vegan Cream
    Cheese 113
History 6

I

Impossible Zucchini Pie 70
Impossible Zucchini
    Pie (photo) 71
Irish Moss 116
Irish Moss Gel 116
Italian Tomato Soup 24

J

Jalapeno Zucchini Fritters 51
Jalapeno Zucchini
    Fritters (photo) 50
Jambalaya 77

K

Kale Burger 78
Kale Burger (photo) 79

L

Lasagna 67
Lasagna (photo) 66

M

Marinara Sauce 67
Mayo 109
Mexican Vegetable Soup 18
Mexican Vegetable Soup (photo) 19
Mylk Bag 124
Moroccan Buckwheat Salad 32
Moroccan Buckwheat
    Salad (photo) 33

N

Nut Mayo 109
Nutrition 11

O

Olive Oil 123
Olive Oil Labeling 123

P

Parsnip Rice 52
"Pasta" Primavera 26
Pesto 40
Picking a Zucchini 7
Pistachio Pudding 90
Pistachio Pudding (photo) 91

Q

Quiche 74

R

Ricotta Cheese Sauce 105

S

Salt 120
Sassy Hot Sauce 114
Sesame Butter 115
Snappy Vegetables 36
Snappy Vegetables (photo) 37
Spice Cake with Green Carob
    Pudding 94
Spice Cake with Green Carob
    Pudding (photo) 87, 95
Spicy Cheese 112
Spicy Nut Cheese 112
Spiralizer 124
Sprouting 121
Sprouting Rice 122
Storing Zucchini 9

Stroganoff 53
Stuffed Zucchini Blossoms 73
Stuffed Zucchini
 Blossoms (photo) 72
Sunflower Greens 24
Sweet Kale Cheesecake 97
Sweet Kale
 Cheesecake (photo) 96

T

Tahini 115
Things to
Do With a Zucchini 13
Tomatoes and Zucchini 44
Tomato Soup, Italian 24
Tuna Salad 31
Tuna Salad (photo) 30
Tuna Wrap 31
Tuna Wrap (photo) 1

V

Vegetable Base 25
Vegetable Noodle Soup 17
Vegetable Noodle
 Soup (photo) 16
Vegetable Ribbon
 Salad (photo) 29
Vegetable Ribbon Salad 28
Vegetables with Creamy
 Mustard 57
Vegetables with Creamy
 Mustard (photo) 56

W

Watermelon 21
Watermelon Soup 21
Watermelon Soup (photo) 20
Wild Jambalaya 77
Wild Jambalaya (photo) 76

Z

Zoodles 48
Zoodle Salad 45
Z Spinach Salad 46
Zucchini Bagels (photo) 107
Zucchini Bagles 106
Zucchini Blossom (photo) 5
Zucchini Blossoms 10
Zucchini Boat 64
Zucchini Boat (photo) 65
Zucchini Carrot
 Bread Sticks 103
Zucchini Carrot
 Bread Sticks (photo) 102
Zucchini Carrot Cake 93
Zucchini Carrot Cake (photo)
 92
Zucchini Casserole 58
Zucchini Casserole (photo) 59
Zucchini Chips 105
Zucchini Chips (photo) 101
Zucchini Cookies 99
Zucchini Crackers 104
Zucchini Marinated
 Vegetables 47
Zucchini Mexicali 43
Zucchini Mexicali (photo) 42
Zucchini Nutrition 11
Zucchini Pizza 86
Zucchini Sticks 85
Zucchini Sticks (photo) 84
Zucchini Vinaigrette 46

About the Author

Kachina Choate is a long-time vegetation who ironically, didn't like vegetables. She stood up one day and said "I'm tired of eating food that tastes like twigs, weeds and styrofoam. There has to be a better way." Since then she has been creating and serving healthy food to her unsuspecting friends who when they find out what they have eaten say "I can't believe I ate something healthy... and liked it!"

She is the author of In the Season Thereof, 101 ½ Raw Zucchinis and What to do With Them, Pumpkins Do Grow on Trees, Thriving on Plant Based Food Storage and Kachina Summer Bear Recipe Card Collection.

She began her natural, unprocessed, raw food journey in 2002, and as a result has recovered from depression and kicked a pernicious sugar addiction. She loves to travel and teach healthy food that tastes good.

She started Summer Bear Life Balance Education, a non-profit organization to help people achieve health and a balanced life.

Website: SummerBear.org

Facebook: SummerBearLifeBalance

Instagram: summer_bear_org

Pinterest:
dollkachina/raw-food-wfpb-food-storage-by-summerbearorg
dollkachina/kachina-summer-bears-raw-foods

www.ingramcontent.com/pod-product-compliance
Lightning Source LLC
Chambersburg PA
CBHW041318110526
44591CB00021B/2828